1895

HEALING THE WOUNDED GOD

On The Hudson

Jung

BOOK SERIES

The Jung on the Hudson Book Series was instituted by the New York Center for Jungian Studies in 1997. This ongoing series is designed to present books that will be of interest to individuals of all fields, as well as mental health professionals, who are interested in exploring the relevance of the psychology and ideas of C. G. Jung to their personal lives and professional activities.

For more information about this series and the New York Center for Jungian Studies contact: Aryeh Maidenbaum, Ph.D., New York Center for Jungian Studies, 41 Park Avenue, Suite ID, New York, NY 10016, telephone (212) 689-8238, fax (212) 889-7634.

For more information about becoming part of this series contact: Nicolas-Hays, P. O. Box 2039, York Beach, ME 03910-2039,

Healing the Wounded God

*finding your personal guide on your
way to individuation and beyond*

JEFFREY RAFF
LINDA BONNINGTON VOCATURA

NICOLAS-HAYS, INC.
York Beach, Maine

First published in 2002 by
NICOLAS-HAYS, INC.
P. O. Box 2039
York Beach, ME 03910-2039

Distributed to the trade by
Red Wheel/Weiser, LLC
P. O. Box 612
York Beach, ME 03910-0612
www.redwheelweiser.com

Library of Congress Cataloging-in-Publication Data
Raff, Jeffrey.
Healing the wounded God : finding your personal guide to individuation
and beyond / Jeffrey A. Raff and Linda Bonnington Vocatura.
p. cm.
Includes bibliographical references and index.
ISBN 0-89254-063-X (alk. paper)
I. Spiritual life—Psychology. 2. Individuation (Psychology)—Religious aspects.
I. Vocatura, Linda Bonnington. II. Title.
BL624 .R323 2002
291.4′4—dc21   2002000282

TCP

Cover art is *The Fall of Icarus*, by Odilon Redon (1840–1916)
Cover and text design by Sky *Peck* Design
Typeset in 11 point Centaur

PRINTED IN CANADA

09 08 06 05 04 03 02
7 6 5 4 3 2 1

CONTENTS

PART I:
THE MYTHOLOGICAL FRAMEWORK FOR THE NEW PARADIGM

PART II:
A PORTRAIT OF THE ALLY

PART III:
A GUIDE FOR THE PROCESS OF HEALING

ACKNOWLEDGMENTS

IN FINISHING THIS BOOK, my first thought and thanks go to Betty Lundsted, who initiated me into the world of publishing with a firm but considerate manner, and whose last conversation with me, before her untimely death, encouraged me to continue my writing of this and future works. Both Linda and I thank Kay Galvan for her comments and suggestions. Finally, my special thanks and love go to my children, Gabe and Rachel, whose support was never lacking, and to my wife and fellow writer, Marilyn, for all her love and companionship.

—J. R.

I WOULD LIKE TO THANK the members of our ally group, who have embarked on the path of spiritual transformations, and who pushed us to write down our teachings about the new paradigm. I am especially grateful to Jane Schwind for her technical support. My sisters, Nancy Bonnington and Ann Louden, provided encouragement for my endeavor at just the right moments. My children, Theresa and Nicholas, have nourished me with unconditional love. Mostly, I am indebted to the constant, loving support of my husband, Michael, who has greatly fostered both my individuation and my creative endeavors.

—L. B. V.

INTRODUCTION

TODAY, MORE THAN EVER, there is a hunger for spiritual connection and fulfillment. As analysts, Linda Vocatura and I see individuals who yearn for deeper truth and who seek not the *idea*, but the *experience* of spirit. They want to perceive directly the forces in the universe that do not belong to the mundane world. We have written a book for the individual seeking a new spiritual path and a new way of comprehending the nature of reality. It is especially written for those who wish to walk this path in their own way and it is our hope that it will serve as a map for those who do so.

For such people, traditional religion as it is practiced today offers scant comfort, and they leave their places of worship with a sense of frustration and lack of fulfillment. Those who turn to New Age writings find ideas and practices that, while intriguing, are superficial and simplistic. Others turn to gurus and the traditions of the East, but many of these individuals come into analysis because something in their soul is still untouched. One client who had been meditating in a Buddhist manner for many years and had experienced "emptiness" came into analysis because her dreams raised the issue of personal relationship with the Divine, creating in her a longing that emptiness could not satisfy. In addition, those who seek to transcend their egos and their feelings in order to conform to such traditions often find themselves depressed and restless.

There are, of course, many paths to union with God, and not all people are dissatisfied with the older traditions. But many are. We are living in a time of spiritual transition as well as a time of spiritual searching. The older models are less satisfying than before, and a new model that might take their place awaits full expression. Linda and I do not intend to disparage the older traditions, but to present a new model that owes much to these earlier systems. There is no question that much of esoteric spirituality relates to many of the characteristics discussed in this book, and we do not hesitate to use some of this older material when appropriate. Yet, taken as a whole, we are presenting something that is new to our age, and may form the contours of the evolution of spirituality for years to come.

A Model of the New Spiritual Paradigm

We have detected the emergence of the new model in the dreams and spiritual experiences of individuals all over the world. Through a careful study of their reports, and through consideration of our own experiences over many years, we have traced the basic features of this new paradigm. We present it in this book not only from a theoretical perspective, but from a practical one as well. Our intent is to convey the idea that a new model for spiritual development exists, which people may experience for themselves. This is by no means a how-to book; it is a study of ideas and possibilities. Those of you who wish to experiment with these possibilities in your own way, and in your own time, will benefit from a look at the model we have presented. Among the most salient features of this model are the following:

PERSONAL IMAGERY

In the first place, people are having experiences that are unique to them, and not collective or universal. Whereas before, images such as Christ or Buddha spoke to the soul of their worshippers, today, seekers experience images of the divine that are more personal to them, that arise from the depths of their own inner world and possess a striking, unique individuality. As one client familiar with Tibetan Buddhist practices told me, "I find more in the images that arise from my own dreams than I do in all the Tibetan Gods and Goddesses I used to meditate on." People who cast their gaze within rather than without are discovering spiritual beings that belong to them and to no others. As they do, they discover a sense of fulfillment, for they have found their own paths, truths, and gods.

PARTNERSHIP WITH THE DIVINE

The second characteristic of the new paradigm is a feeling of deep love and partnership between the spiritual being and the individual. As individuals discover their own unique incarnations of the Divine, they discover that they love these figures, and even more startling, that these beings love them. There is no longer room for a sense of worship and devotion to a higher power that one must follow and obey; on the contrary, there is the sense that God is seeking us with the same intensity that we are seeking It. God does not wish to reign as a remote king on a heavenly throne, but wishes to be with us in our everyday world and to partner us in our lives. Moreover, God needs us, and in this need, we find purpose and meaning.

AN INDIVIDUATING GOD WHO NEEDS US

The third attribute of the new paradigm is that God is far from perfect.

God is not an omnipotent being sitting in judgment of our defects. God, too, is lacking and, far from judging us, needs us to heal Its wounds. The first few chapters of this book will detail this heavenly imperfection. For now, it is enough to know that the way we perceive God is altering profoundly. We now see an individual and individuating God, an imperfect and needy God, who manifests as a unique being in search of Its own truth and fulfillment. We see a God who needs human beings in order to become whole, as human beings need It in order to gain their own wholeness. These perceptions are dramatically different from the collective religious views of God, and different even from older, mystical views of the Divine.

Active Imagination and Experience of the Psychoid

These insights are not based on philosophical thought or scholarly exegesis, but on real, living experiences. And so the fourth attribute of the new model is that it is based on direct experiences. These experiences come through the technique called active imagination. It was C. G. Jung who rediscovered this method of experiencing the imaginal realms, but it is an ancient one that was known to both the Sufis and the alchemists. Active imagination consists of quieting the mind and allowing images to arise. Once these images have arisen, the ego interacts with them. These images personify the many different aspects of the unconscious psyche, and by interacting with them, the ego makes them conscious and both transforms and is transformed by them. As we shall see later, active imagination provides the means for manifesting the human Self. Jung felt that active imagination was the most effective means of experiencing the unconscious and speeding the process of individuation.

Through our research and experiences, we have discovered that active imagination allows us to perceive the world of the unconscious, and to experience a world beyond the psyche. We have termed this world the "psychoid," and it is the fifth attribute of the new paradigm. We argue that a world exists that is neither the mundane world nor the inner psychic world, but a world external to the psyche and yet other than the ordinary. There are spiritual entities and forces that one can experience in the psychoid realm through active imagination. We shall discuss the nature of the psychoid realm at length, but for now, we wish only to emphasize the existence of a transpsychic reality and of transpsychic entities.

The Ally and Ego Transformation

Among the many denizens of the psychoid world, the most important is the ally. The ally constitutes the sixth dimension of the new model. It is a psychoidal being that is divine in its own right, though separate from both the human Self and God. It is through the ally that the human and Divine come into union. As a divine being, the ally seeks partnership and transformation. It forms a loving relationship with its human partner and guides its partner on the path to individuation and, ultimately, union with God.

The ally is one aspect of the Divine, but there are two other aspects of the Divine, which we call the human-Divine and the God-Divine. In the new paradigm, the human being takes on a high status. He or she possesses within him- or herself a divine center that Jung termed the Self, but which we call the human-Divine. Every person is at the core a god-like being capable of deepest wisdom and insight, and of uniting with the other aspects of the Divine.

In addition, unlike so many other traditions, the new model does not reject the ego nor call for its elimination or submersion in the Divine. Rather, it calls for a revised and transformed ego, shed of its more unconscious and base characteristics, but strengthened by seeing who and what it really is. Without the human ego, the human Self never manifests. Without the human Self, the ally cannot unite with the human being. And unless the ally unites with the human being, it cannot bring the human-Divine into union with the God-Divine. The God-Divine is the twin of the human-Divine and both belong to each other. It is through the efforts of the human being and the agency of the ally that the restoration of the human- and the God-Divine takes place. When they are united with each other and with the ally, the divinity is whole and we term the whole divinity the Divine-Divine. Once the Divine-Divine comes into being, the ally unites with it to form a unified being we have termed "EO."

HEALING THE TRIUNE DIVINITY

The seventh aspect of the new model is that the Divinity is split into three parts: ally, human-Divine, and God-Divine. It is also part of the model that these three aspects need to unite with each other, and that this unification takes place through the ally. The ally can only accomplish this task with the help of a human partner.

In the new paradigm, the human being is potentially the means by which God finds Its own wholeness. The redemption of an imperfect God, an imperfect Cosmos, and an imperfect human being are all aspects of this model. This redemption first requires the union of the ally with its human partner. The ally then helps the human-Divine unite with the God-Divine, forming a new entity, the Divine-Divine, a new unified divinity. The ally then unites with the Divine-Divine, creating EO. Through the processes whereby these unions are created, the human being, the ally, and God all undergo transformations. Uniting the Divinity is not an easy task to accomplish and yet it is a rewarding and fulfilling one that gives individuals a central role in the evolution of the universe.

Other traditions possessed some of these aspects but, to our knowledge, none of them possessed them all. Put together, these aspects create a unique spiritual path. Through the practice of active imagination, an individual discovers his or her own inner divine nature, encounters the ally and other spirits of the psychoid, and unites with God. He or she finds the means to cultivate a whole new perception of reality and his or her place within it, a place of honor, rich with meaning and responsibility.

In the pages that follow we shall present this new spiritual paradigm from a number of perspectives. Making use of mythology, both old and new, we discuss the symbolism that depicts the ally, the psychoid realm, and the work of uniting with the ally and with God. We explore the different aspects of the Divinity and the creation myths that reveal the split that exists among these aspects. We turn to the symbolism of alchemy to portray the nature of the ally, and to help create a model for the actual relationship with it. In the chapter on working with the ally we describe how to use active imagination to experience the ally directly. We present a map of the various stages of working with an ally, from the very beginning to the deepest states of ecstatic union when EO emerges. We also discuss the ways in which the ally differs from and is like the experience of angels, a topic of great interest today. Reaching into the past, while interpreting with the eyes of the present, helps to ground our concepts in the psychic history of humanity.

Linda and I have spent the last eighteen years working together and exploring the ally and the new paradigm of which it is part. We have meditated, done active imagination, studied old texts and myths, read contemporary works on spirituality and worked with hundreds of students. The explication of the new model derives from all of these resources. We did not rely on our own visionary experience alone, but added to it intellectual study and the observation of the experiences of others, both students and non-students. Finally, we have written nothing that we have not experienced for ourselves, believing that models of spiritual transformation must not emerge from intuition or intellect alone. They must be founded on experience, or their value lies in speculation only. We offer the new paradigm not as conjecture, but as our best expression of real experience. It is our hope that in doing so we make it easier for you to gain your own experience and to add your own contribution to the paradigm currently emerging from the depths of the psyche.

PART ONE

The Mythological Framework for the New Paradigm

Chapter 1

THE WORLD BEYOND THE PSYCHE

OFTEN PEOPLE CONTACT ME to begin dream work because of early childhood experiences or dreams that have haunted them for most of their lives. This is exactly how I got started on a path that has led me into the exploration of the psychoid. When I was only 3 1/2 years old, I awoke one night, sensing a great pressure on my chest. As I opened my eyes, I discovered a very tall, ethereal being at the side of my bed. Sheer terror tore through me, but I was quickly calmed by the soothing effect this night visitor conveyed and the pressure on my chest was relieved as the visitor lifted its hand off of me. I was bathed in the most amazing, loving warmth emanating from this ethereal stranger. And then, the stranger was gone. I was left with a mystery that only as an adult have I been able to comprehend through the aid of C. G. Jung's work on the psyche and through my collaborative work with Jeff Raff.

I have come to understand my early encounter as an experience of the psychoid: that dimension in which both matter and spirit exist as one in a supercharged, living, autonomous, otherworldly form. No matter how often my parents, or priests, or relatives tried to tell me that my guardian angel was produced by an overly active imagination, I knew intuitively that their conclusion was not the answer to this mystery. I soon quit sharing the experience with anyone, although it continued to haunt me into my adult years.

Despite the fact that Jung did an immense amount of research on the psyche, he has left the investigation of the psychoid to us: "Unfortunately, these things [psychoidal] have been far too little investigated. This is a task for the future."[1] Jeff and I have taken on this task and have constructed the beginnings of a model for the psychoid and its center, the ally.

The Trap of the Closed System Theory of the Psyche

I began to investigate my experience with Jung's *Structure and Dynamics of the Psyche*. Reading it for the third time, it suddenly became clear that I was stumbling over ideas because I did not accept his closed system theory of the psyche. Jung based his model on the idea that there is a fixed amount of energy in the psyche (psychic energy, or *libido*, as termed in psychology), which changes form without ever changing quantity. Simply put, when we are conscious of something, that "something" has acquired enough energy to rise out of or be pulled from the unconscious; at the same time, that which consciousness is no longer focused on loses energy and sinks back into the unconscious. We can never achieve total consciousness within the closed system theory of the psyche. This theory describes a system dependent upon dominance, which creates a tension with its opposite, non-dominance. Of course, this makes complete sense to me rationally and is, after all, the premise of some sciences. I had studied the sciences in college as a pre-med major and never once questioned the closed system theory. Why I decided to question it, God only knows. But now, the idea of such limitations shocks me at an intuitive level, perhaps because so many clients tell me they are not able to change, or that they can only go so far, due to "human limitations." Somewhere within me the premise of limitations, or a model based upon limitations, was repugnant.

I now realize that my reaction came from an "unconscious" awareness of the dire ramifications to an existence within such an energy model: it curtails growth and ultimately threatens life. There is also a collectively-expressed desire for peace within both the individual and the world. However, the dynamics of a closed energy system require tension rather than peace. In theory, the combined energy value of all components must always equal the original absolute energy quantity. If one thing vies for energy, another thing must give it up. This creates tension and an eternal tug-of-war. Force, a measurement of energy, results from this tension, without which there is no energy. Dominance is the rule of thumb. If everything were to take on an absolute equal value, there would no longer be tension or force, and energy would cease to exist. At best, such a closed system becomes completely static. There can be no growth. Life, itself, would then eventually cease, as it cannot exist without dynamic energy. So in order to maintain a fixed energy situation, one life form must be given up for another. In a perpetual cycle, the growth of one needs to be given up so that another may survive. This idea is expressed collectively in the recycling/rebirth/reincarnation motif. Or, as Joseph Campbell so aptly put it, "Life lives on lives."[2] To truly reap our wish for peace and to open the opportunity for uncurtailed growth, we would need an outside source of energy in order to overcome the dynamics of a closed world.

The Creation Myths and the Psychoid

You can imagine my dismay when I was led by the voice of inner wisdom into the stories of creation mythology, only to discover that the world (analogous in this mythology to the psyche) is indeed closed. There is, however, a redeeming facet to those stories that allude to life or to energy outside the enclosed realm. Creation mythology, I realized, would be an excellent framework for the understanding of the psychoid. Some of these stories follow, as a way of visualizing our predicament. While I note my sources for the stories throughout this book, these stories are a common heritage of humankind, and so I will tell them in my own words, in the tradition of storytelling.

The Icelandic story of the giant, Ymir, and the god, Odin, begins with a yawning abyss from which all creation evolves.[3] The first beings to emerge from this abyss are Ymir, and a cow that nurses him. Ymir then fathers the giants, while the cow, by licking an ice block, uncovers the first god, Buri. Eventually, jealousy causes a great battle between the gods and giants in which Odin, a third generation god, slays Ymir. In fact, all the first generation giants are slain by the gods, except for one giant and his wife, who escape to form a new race.

Odin, now leader of the gods, fashions the world from the body of Ymir; his skull becomes the vault of heaven, while his body becomes Earth. Odin then places the Moon, Sun, and stars beneath the vault and, with his brothers, completes creation, including the creation of human beings. The myth goes on to describe an end to the gods, when the vault of heaven will crack. At such a time, the world will be renewed by the arrival of new gods already in existence but never before known, since they have been on the other side of the vault. These new, unknown, enti-ties are most likely the progeny of the escaped couple.

So, while life exists within a confined world, it also exists outside that world. Two other myths with similar motifs exist. In the Wichita tribe, the highest God is called "Man Never Known on Earth,"[4] and in a Cherokee myth, the highest place is known as Galun'lati, " beyond the arch."[5] Both of these allude to an unknown life outside our world, or in other words, beyond our psyche. This unknown life provides an addi-tional source of energy other than our psyche's.

Several other myths describe the sealing of our world by a vault. In the Egyptian version, the god, Ra, grows angry at human ingratitude and demands to be taken on Nut's back into the vault of Heaven, beyond human reach.[6] In the Chinese myth of P'an Ku, this god's skull becomes the dome of the sky.[7] The Icelandic Ymir experienced a similar fate. A Cherokee story describes the sky vault as solid rock. While in the Hebrew *Sepher Yetzirah*, Yahveh chooses three from among the simple letters and forms them into the great Name of IHV, which seals the universe.[8] In Genesis, God creates a vault to divide the waters above from the waters below. He then calls the vault Heaven and creates a universe within the waters below it.[9] The image of water is also seen in the Rig Veda: "the creator having first fastened the extreme ends, spread out heaven and earth between them. . . . the waters as the two ends of the universe."[10]

One must not overlook the fact that both humans and the gods live within the enclosure, so the waters above or outside of the world/uni-verse remain a mystery to us. Keep in mind that what lies outside the vault contains the same creative material as that which lies within the vault, since it all began as one undivided, living potential. The initial stage of a complete creation myth, such as the Icelandic or Gnostic, always begins with descriptions of an "original" life material: be it an abyss, water, light, or "not-being." This first stage exists before creation, and is reflective of creation being pregnant with itself. So, before creation, there is an additional life-energy available for the enclosed world.

These myths describe the formation of a bounded world, separating it from an unbounded realm. It is this unbounded dimension that exists outside the created universe, where the unknown and new gods live, that we are naming the psychoid. This differs from Jung's identification of the psychoid, which, in these myths, would be the bounded area within which gods and goddesses reside. Jung named this bounded area "the collective unconscious," and equated it to the psychoid. Our definition explains the profound impact of experiences charged with unbounded energy and bringing with them the feel of a unique, alive alien being, unlike any psychic image. A life energy truly exists beyond our closed universe, which may account for the concerted efforts by many to discover life beyond our own world, or, in some people's belief, that aliens exist. There is a trace of psychological truth to these collective ideas.

The creation myths provide a means of envisioning this concept wherein the enclosed world represents our psyche. The boundary of our enclosed world that is the abode of the gods and goddesses is Jung's collective unconscious. It is a deposit of accumulated human experiences bundled into several motifs, such as witch, savior, mother, and father. These are then masked in the faces of gods and giants and defined by Jung as the archetypes. So each archetype embodies a particular motif formed through the history of human experience and takes on an autonomous personality. Many truths have been given to us by the archetypes; that is to say the gods and goddesses, in their powerfully autonomous manner, have persuaded us to accept those truths as absolute. Keep this in mind as we continue with the creation myths, because you will discover that some of our historically upheld beliefs are based on distortion and falsehood.

The Bounded Realm

In addition to the power of the gods (archetypes), the strength of the collective unconscious is also reflected in the myth's description of the world's boundary as being impenetrable, regardless of the material from which it is constructed. Depending on the myth, this material might be rock, skull, body, or a veil. Even a veil can become a formidable boundary, as seen in the Swahili story, where a carpet of many-colored veils acts as the boundary. Beneath the carpet, in its shadow, the soul resides.

The Gnostic creation story also describes a veiled boundary that separates the psyche from the psychoid.[11] Like the Icelandic myth, it describes a rending of the boundary. Sophia, a second-generation divine entity, flows out of the first generation entity, Pistis. Sophia wishes a work of heavenly likeness. In other words, she desires a re-creation of Heaven. This wish creates a veil with light above and shadow below. Sophia's disturbance over the production of a shadow causes the birth of the androgynous being, Yaldoboath. He rises out of Chaos, which exists within the shadow. Sophia brings Yaldoboath to life and instructs him to create order out of Chaos. She then withdraws, leaving Yaldoboath to believe that he is the first and only god. Sophia actually exists as a divine entity outside the closed world. She is not a divinity of the closed world.

Remember the concept of false beliefs passed on by an archetype? Yaldoboath is such an archetype. He gives birth to the Authorities, who are second generation gods, and they in turn create people. Yaldoboath then impresses upon the people that there is only one god and this one god, by the way, lives within the closed system. The idea of an outside creator is not communicated to the people. The emergence of the original divinity, Sophia-Pistis, or the Icelandic Ymir, initiates creation with their differentiation from the original pregnant material. This truth about creation is oftentimes kept secret from humans. Humans' ignorance of such activity, along with the impressiveness of the formed boundary, leaves us with a sense of having no recourse to our fate; we live within limits. We then fall prey to feelings of being stuck, crippling our aspirations for growth. No wonder I reacted as I did to Jung's libido theory! Fortunately, in the Icelandic and Gnostic myths, I found some hope prophesied for people. Sophia, in the meantime, has become angered by Yaldoboath's declaration of primacy and sends her first prophecy: "An enlightened, immortal man exists before you. This will appear within your molded bodies . . . all of the deficiency which appeared . . . will be dissolved."[12] Yaldoboath, of course, wants to see this person, and is granted by Sophia an image of Light Adam, the enlightened immortal, within which is seen a human likeness that will purify the deficiency.

This imagery of Light Adam within which a human likeness exists is a wonderful twofold description: the Self is Light Adam and the ego within is human likeness. In her book, *On Dreams and Death*, Marie-Louise Von Franz shared a dream in which the dreamer experienced being a little ball or sphere inside of a larger ball. This closely resembles the Gnostic imagery. Von Franz used it as an example of the Self-ego relationship, where the Self is the center of the psyche and is also the psyche's potential wholeness, while the ego is the center of consciousness and is also consciousness itself. Without the ego there is no consciousness.

A Hawaiian myth poetically portrays human identity with consciousness in the statement, "Man was here now; it was Day."[13] According to the Gnostic message, consciousness is key to rectifying the derailment of creation. Also, according to its message, we actually have two centers, the ego and the Self, which must somehow come into relationship for a harmonious life experience. The formation of this Self-ego relationship produces a transformed consciousness. Jung defined this formation as the individuation process.

Recall in the closed energy theory that if two things acquire equal energy value (which is a picture of harmony), then tension and energy, itself, would cease to exist. Therefore, for the ideal relationship of harmony to exist, an additional energy source must be found. This energy source can be acquired from the original pregnant material found in the psychoid, or unbounded realm.

Escaping the Bounded Realm

The Gnostic myth continues to describe a storm of creation infused with plots in which the Authorities deceive people, so we will not know our true identity. Sophia is furious at these events and seals her Heaven with a veil. Pistis, the boundless one, out of which Sophia arose, sends blessed little angels to reveal knowledge and truth to humans in order to expose the Authorities. Their exposure leads to a series of events that are propelled by Sophia's wrath. The world will be shaken by great thunder, rulers will lament their deaths, kings will make war with one another, the

Sun will darken, and stars will disregard their course. She will drive out the Authorities and all will collapse, so that light will replace darkness and the glory of the Unbegotten will appear, ushering in a kingless realm.

A type of apocalypse is described with light, or consciousness, overtaking darkness, or unconsciousness. The little angels, which can be thought of as energies outside the boundary, provide what is necessary for the attainment of a harmonious Self-ego relationship and, thus, transformed consciousness. This transformation was impossible within a closed psyche or system, while the quantity of energy remained constant. The kingless realm refers to an unlimited quantity of energy where dominance and tension—conditions of a closed energy system—cease. The kingless realm is centered not upon Authority figures, but rather upon the transcended Self-ego that is freed consciousness. The Unbegotten, representing what we define as the ally, are those forms that have evolved from the pregnant material outside of the boundary, while humans have evolved inside it.

The Birth of New Consciousness

The gods, descendents of the Divine, invested a tremendous amount of energy into the making of enclosures. The Divine, who is the original entity, emerged from the pregnant material and was shut out by these enclosures for the remainder of creation. There must have been some practical reason for this, if in fact, life instinctively seeks continuation. It is interesting to note that creation stories always end when people are formed, so it seems that human creation is the mythological goal. This makes sense in terms of the Gnostic story in which the person becomes key to the overthrowing of the Authorities in order to know the truth of themselves. Most of what is created prior to humans is for the assurance of their survival after birth. The enclosed world actually serves as a womb, pregnant with consciousness.

As with any pregnancy, the natural occurrence of birth must take place in order to prevent death. If a fetus does not emerge, it and, possibly, its mother will die. The womb must open for the purpose of transformation via the acquisition of additional energy. The process of opening defines evolution. Evolution is the solution to the tension within a closed system where energy constantly circles round and round. Jung expressed the plight of a bounded world: "Always we shall have to begin again from the beginning."[14] He was referring to the effort (energy) of becoming whole or, in other words, the manifestation of the Self-ego, one's intended, authentic nature. This realization requires evolution, or the opening of our enclosure to the energy of the psychoid. Thus, we need our closed environment to collapse, as was prophesied in the Icelandic and Gnostic myths. As the fetus in a closed system, our gestation period must end. We must focus upon our birth, our evolution.

Why are we not expending great effort toward this goal? Instead, we find ourselves in the unfortunate position of stagnation as described in this Sufi tale: While walking with friends, a Sufi teacher witnesses a person cutting down a tree. The Sufi turns to the friends, saying, "See this branch, so full of sap? It is happy, because it is unaware of what has happened to it. Eventually, this branch will discover that it has been cut off. In the meantime, it will not listen to the truth you tell it. This condition of ignorance and severance, this is the condition of people."[15]

The answer is twofold: first, we are severed from and made blind to the Divine by staying within our boundary. Second, we have been misled by the gods into believing that we do not have the potential to break through those boundaries. We make a distinction here between "Divine" and "gods." The Divine is the original entity of creation and exists in the psychoid, or the boundless realm, whereas the gods are descendants of the Divine and live within the closed system.

The mythological terms of "Divine," "Unbegotten," or "Unknown," which we have called the "ally," symbolize the Psychoid Self. The Psychoid Self is a center that unites both psyche (our bounded selves) and psychoid (the boundless realm). For wholeness, our ego-Self consciousness must become related to the Psychoid Self. As consciousness interacts with the Psychoid Self (the ally), it derives tremendous feelings of energy, freedom, and eternity.

The boundary that shuts off our sight of the Psychoid Self (ally) threatens our lives because we cannot free ourselves from the closed world alone. The Psychoid Self provides the energy boost needed for our birth from the closed world, thus preventing our death. The Psychoid Self also holds knowledge of our true potentialities that we need in order to overcome the boundary. The boundary is breached by building an ego-Self-ally axis that brings about a transfiguration into an immortal entity. This happens quite naturally, as unbounded life energy is acquired through the process. The details of this axis building are the subject matter of chapters 4 and 5.

Challenging the Boundary

The collective notion of an inherent danger in challenging the boundary brings about another problem to overcome: a problem of fear and an assumption of impossibility. In the Cherokee story, "The Door

Through the Sky,"[16] seven men begin a journey to the Sun, only to discover that the sky is solid. As they wonder what to do, the sky vault opens, creating a doorway to the other side of the sky through which the Sun emerges. The men jump back, except for one, who decides to leap through the opening only to be crushed as the door closes. The other six men assume the task is too risky and return home, never to see the face of the Sun.

The implication here is that to challenge the boundary brings about death. The men never see the face of the Sun, which is similar to the Western tradition of never looking into the face of God for fear of being burned to ashes. Jung actually warns us to avoid an early death by "living in harmony with the habitus of our ancestral psychic life . . . by conforming to it one has a reasonable life expectancy."[17] Ancestral psychic life refers to the archetypes that reside within the boundary of the closed realm. Hence, to stay in harmony with ancestral psychic life (or to stay in harmony with the archetypes) would keep one within the bounded realm. According to Jung, if we breach this harmony, we risk an early death. Most people fear death and avoid it all costs. However, as witnessed in the Gnostic myth, often the archetypes intend to deceive us. This fear can keep us forever severed from the psychoid.

Instead, the Hopi "Myth of Emergence" extends a way of accessing the psychoid.[18] In this story, creation begins as Endless Space in which exists the creator, Taiowa, who begets Sotaknang, the "first power," and nephew to Taiowa. Taiowa instructs his nephew on how to lay out the universe in proper order. The nephew then gathers what is to be solid and fashions nine kingdoms: one for Taiowa, one for himself, and seven for life to come. Sotaknang then creates Her, who embodies knowledge, wisdom, and love, and who is to remain on Earth as a helper. Through her creation song she creates all on Earth. She then molds four humans in the image of the nephew. The humans are told to look through the face of the Sun to their original father, Taiowa.

Taiowa, as the original entity, is the Divine, and, although removed from humanity, he can be accessed if certain instructions are followed. Sotaknang asks only that humans respect and love the creator as they communicate with him by use of their vibratory centers, the heart and throat, and through the "open door," that is the soft spot on top of their heads. Gradually, however, the people forget and use the centers for earthly purposes so that harmony is lost. Harmony can exist here since there is a flow of energy through the open door from the Divine. The few who continue to use the vibratory centers are saved from destruction, and re-emerge into a rearranged Earth. In other words, consciousness has been changed.

A second time, the world leads people to trouble with its greed for goods and, a second time, those who sing the song of creation are saved only to re-emerge with a reminder to stay focused upon Taiowa. But cities and civilizations grow and breed discord that leads humans to attack each other.

So, for a third time, those who have kept the song in their hearts re-emerge from destruction and are instructed on how they may arrive at yet a fourth world, guided by inner wisdom through the door at the top of their heads. Each must make a flat boat and go alone through the open door, guided by spirits, to the place of emergence. (One cannot help but see the similarity here to the Egyptian journey through the underworld in order for the soul to be reborn.) Each person is to follow his or her own star until it stops, and there, he or she is to settle. The third world will be brought into the fourth world, if the people preserve memory and the meaning of their emergence.

The Divine Connection

The Hopi myth expresses a desire for humans to stay focused beyond their enclosed system. The boundary remains open to those who use the door. The maintenance of a Divine connection becomes the key to survival and eventual freedom. The quantity of life energy never becomes fixed as long as the open door is used to access the Divine. The barrier actually lies within us and is activated when the ego falls prey to temptations of vanity, greed, and power, occupying us so that we no longer communicate from our vibratory centers. These temptations are actually the same as those motivating the mythic gods who led violent overthrows of the original divinities and deceived human beings. (We will soon discuss them in detail.)

The theme of the open door at the top of the head is similar to the Cherokee "door through the sky" and the Hopi theme of looking through the Sun to Taiowa. Opening doors is a metaphor that was also used in the Mithraic Mystery Religion's liturgical passages, which describe the ascent of the soul through a series of doors to their highest God.

[The soul is instructed to announce itself in order for events to unfold.] I am a star. . . . Immediately after you have said these things the sun's disk will be expanded . . . you will see many five-pronged stars coming forth. . . . [Another series of prayers are invoked.] After saying this, you will see the doors thrown open [more prayers open doors to reveal the Fates and gods, culminating in an encounter with the highest God] . . . look in the air and you will see . . . a god descending . . . with a white tunic and a golden crown. [19]

Again, the idea is of going beyond the Sun, beyond the created realm into the psychoid, where entities, who were never of this world, exist along with the first origin, the Divine. The stars refer to the immortals and represent exactly the transformation that occurs when the ego follows the Self through the open door to its Self in the psychoid. In other words, humans have become fully conscious of who they really are. They see their immortality. The star symbolizes the eternal aspect of man. In the *Egyptian Book of the Dead*, a soul passes through gates beyond the gods to become a star, "behold thy soul is a star living,[20] . . . he rises in his place like a star."[21] The "star living" is consciousness of immortality. In other words, we achieve knowledge of existence beyond the finite material body.

This idea is expressed in the Hopi Myth of Emergence as bringing the third world into the fourth. The description of moving out of the body into the fourth world may lead to the assumption that the third world is connected to the body, or the material world. The body is often associated with the ego, and the ego is directly related to consciousness. Also, preserving memory is a function of the ego and, therefore, a function of consciousness. Hence, to bring the third into the fourth is synonymous with having the ego-Self exist in the endless rather than die. Consciousness thus remains intact for this final transition, assuring the transcendence of consciousness beyond the closed realm. Recall that in the myths, the human being seems to have been the purpose of creation, and the enclosed world is a womb for our eventual birth. Since human beings symbolize consciousness, and consciousness, in this Hopi myth, emerges beyond the closed world, it would appear that creation's purpose has been fulfilled.

Reference to the third world as being body (or material) alludes to yet another element in the idea of bringing the third into the fourth. The final transformation brings the material into the spiritual realm. An analogy to this "mixture of matter and spirit" (matter being represented by the third world and spirit by the fourth) is the nature of light, which is both wave and particle. A newly-created immortal body, similar to the concept of a subtle body, then exists in this fourth-combined-with-third world.

The Gods' Deception

Story after story exists about humans being misled by the gods as to what our purpose and status are. So, in addition to the boundary problem, we have this second hurdle to overcome to fulfill creation's purpose of evolution. In order to evolve, consciousness must be born from its fetal (closed) psychic state. The Gnostic myth revealed the gods' deceptive behavior, as does this Venezuelan myth:[22]

The supreme divinity, Wanadi, lives in a Heaven of boundless light. This light gave birth to life when there was no door between Heaven and Earth like there is now. Wanadi desired to make people on Earth, but because he never leaves Heaven, he instead sent his spirit, Damodede. The first attempt created Odo'sha, who was covered with hair and wanted to rule the Earth, and so became jealous of

Damodede. (This is similar to Yaldoboath's jealousies in wanting to be the absolute power.) From jealousy, Odo'sha misled the first people by telling them lies about the Earth being his and by teaching them to kill. In punishment for listening to Odo'sha, the people were turned into animals. Psychologically, this means that consciousness was lost to the unconsciousness of instincts.

Consciousness was threatened by the antics of Odo'sha, so a second Damodede attempted to rectify the mistake by populating Earth with people and showing them that death was only a trick of Odo'sha. The Damodede brought a great ball of heavy shells, within which the people awaited their birth. He created an elaborate plan to dispel the myth of death, and by doing so, he left three things with a helper: his chakara, the holder of his power; his tobacco; and night. He warned this helper never to play with his chakara. Of course, his warnings, through some trickery of Odo'sha, went unheeded and night descended on the world. Odo'sha prevented the people's emergence from the huge ball of shells. Once again, unconsciousness prevailed. The unborn, screaming in fear, needed to wait for Odo'sha's death in order to be born.

In the meantime, a third Damodede, in disguise, managed to populate Earth as we know it today. Creation, however, is not complete since the unborn still wait to emerge and the door to Heaven remains closed.

The unborn represent a consciousness that can only be realized by piercing through the illusion of Odo'sha, an archetype (or god within our enclosed system). We must accept the fact that an archetype can have malicious intent even though that archetype may be our own creator. The illusion that needs to be broken is the belief that only our bounded world, or only the psyche, exists. If, instead, we can begin to absorb and accept the idea that life-energy (Wanadi) exists outside of us in the psychoid realm, consciousness will begin its journey (birth from the ball of shells) toward freedom.

In Christian mythology, Christ talks about consciousness (man) breaking away from two prominent archetypes: "For I have come to set a man against his father, and a daughter against her mother. . . . A man's enemies will be those of his own household."[23] Our "enemies" are the archetypes of the collective unconscious and our "household" is our psyche. Christ's intent here is for consciousness to free itself from ancestral, patterned thought and behavior in order to focus upon God, similar to maintaining a focus on Taiowa of the Hopi myth.

The folly of following archetypal patterns is poignantly presented in the Mesopotamian story of Adapa,[24] the first human, who is instructed by his father Ea, the god of wisdom, on how to successfully respond to the gods in order to pass through the gates of heaven: "You must flatter the first two gods, then refuse the bread and water offered to you by Anu. But, you may put on the robes offered." Adapa follows his father's advice. Anu, the high god, asks Adapa, "Why have you acted so strangely?" And, Adapa tells Anu that he was simply following the advice of his father. Anu then declares, "In so doing, you have passed up the gift of immortality!"

Keeping human beings from immortality sustains the cyclical pattern of our closed system and prevents the continued growth of consciousness. Even God, as spoken in Genesis, acts to prevent our full development:

See, the man has become like one of us, with his knowledge of good and evil. He must not be allowed to stretch his hand out next and pick from the tree of life also, and eat some and live forever.[25]

He then posts the cherubs and flaming swords to guard the tree of life. God robs us of our due inheritance of immortality, in accordance with archetypal intentions. Christian mythology teaches that God resides in heaven. In an earlier quote from Genesis, Heaven is described as being within the vault that divides the waters. The vault and the waters under the vault represent the enclosed, created world. Therefore, God resides within the closed realm and is an archetype. The gods within the created, closed world represent archetypes. And the archetypes' deceptiveness fuels an energy that repels a person from the boundary, as seen in both Genesis and in the Cherokee "Door Through the Sky."

Duty to the Archetypes

In addition to this, when humans are created their purpose and status are scripted for them. Generally, humans are instructed to be good, to sacrifice, and to serve, respect, adore, and show gratitude toward the creator. In the Eskimo myth, Raven, the creator, informs the people, "I am your Father and to me you owe the land you have and your being, and you must never forget me."[26] In some myths, there is a demand for gratitude, even if human creation is accidentally accomplished. Zeus banishes people to a life of ignorance, fear, worship, and sacrifice to the gods. In Genesis, God expels humans from Eden to "till the soil." In both the Gnostic and Swahili stories, God created humans to be his servants. And, in both Summerian and Mesopotamian myths, the gods neglect their duties, then command people to do their labor. Overcoming these dictates might not be so difficult, except that the creator often destroys people when they do not perform. This fear of retribution inhibits our focus, since we must attend to maintaining peace with the gods in order to ensure survival. Aspiring to the Divine, beyond the realm of these gods, seems too risky. The gods, symbols of the archetypes of the collective unconscious, thus manage to keep a status quo. Human scripting, because it comes from the collective, archetypal unconscious, has a powerful impact on our behavior.

An Italian tale, "The Land Where One Never Dies," follows the struggles of a young man who sets off in search of such a land.[27] He departs after farewells to family and friends. After much travel, he meets an old man pushing a wheelbarrow full of rocks. The young man asks him about the land where one never dies. This old man says that if he sticks with him for one hundred years, until the mountain is carted away, he will not die. The young man dismisses this advice saying, "This is no place for me," and continues on his journey until he comes across another old man pruning branches. The youth repeats his question, to which the old man replies that if he stays with him until all the trees in the forest are trimmed he will live for two hundred years. Once again, the young man says, "No," and continues the journey. He comes to a third old man who is watching a duck drink seawater. The youth repeats his question and this old man offers three hundred years of life. "No, no, no!" says the youth. He travels onward until he stumbles across a magnificent palace. Another old man answers his knock at the door. This time, when he asks the same question, he is told that he has found the land where one never dies. The youth moves into the palace and lives in bliss for centuries.

One day, however, the young man is driven by a strong desire to visit his family. Reluctantly, the old man warns the youth to stay upon his gift of a white horse and never to dismount the horse or he will die. Upon returning home, and as he had been forewarned, the youth sees that hundreds of years have changed his village beyond recognition. Disappointed, he turns back toward the palace.

On his return trip, he comes upon an old man with a cart, full of shoes, that is stuck in the mud. The man begs the youth for help. The young man, taking pity on the old man, disregards his instructions. He dismounts the white horse to help the old man with the cart. As soon as the youth's foot touches the ground, the old man grabs him, and announces, "I am Death!" The young man dies.

Here, the lure of attachment to family (an archetype) is fatal. Images or ideas of family, pulling on a person's memory, can eventually gain enough energy to draw that person (the youth) away from his Self (the land where one never dies). Attending to the pull of archetypes ultimately leads one into the hands of death. Therefore, if we do not break away from "ancestral psychic life," our life expectancy is shorter than it would have been had we kept our attention on the instructions given us in the palace beyond the closed world. That old man's warnings can be likened to Christ's reference to "the foes of the household." If the youth had been willing to stay away from his ancestral home or turn away from the ancestor (the old man with the cart in the mud), he would not have come to such a tragic end.

The young man's really tragic flaw is the feeling of pity that takes him from his horse. The word, pity, comes from the Latin *pietas*, meaning "duty to God." Remember that human experience, as told in mythic stories, includes man's destruction by the gods should he disregard his duties to them. An accumulation of tasks attached to pity (duty to God) creates an energy capable of dislodging one from his ego-Self axis (consciousness). Our youth, in this story, does not overcome his survival instinct of avoiding punishment by performing. In order to avoid death, he would have had to invest an offsetting amount of energy into not pitying but, rather, to staying on the horse. This change in behavior would take heroic effort of will.

Such effort of will is hard to achieve. In a Japanese tale the fisherman, Taro, rescues and befriends a turtle.[28] This tale repeats the Italian theme: Taro's turtle carries him far, far away beneath the sea to the Sea King's Palace, where all four seasons exist together. There, he discovers the turtle's true identity as the King's daughter and they are married. He lives in a peace and bliss he has never before experienced, until one day when he awakens to realize who he is and that he does not belong in this magnificent palace. He tells his wife that he must leave the palace and return to his old home. She reluctantly agrees, giving him a gift that he must never open until he reunites with her. Then she carries him back to the place where she first met him and he returns home. Home has changed with the passing of three hundred years and he realizes his mistake in returning there. Heartbroken, Taro returns to the sea and not knowing what to do, opens the gift. He immediately ages and dies.

In this story, as in the Italian tale, the peace, bliss, and immortality achieved when the person reaches that distant, otherworldly location (the psychoid) are forsaken in order to heed an archetypal lure that pulls consciousness back into the unconscious. The human assumption of unworthiness, as expressed by Taro's statement that he does not belong in the magnificent palace, is rooted once more in human creation. We have been told by the gods that our role is one of servitude and ingratiation. This keeps our focus within the boundary and our consciousness continually collapsing into unconsciousness. Taro's final failing is his loss of memory regarding the box. Memory is an ego function. The ego's lack of ability to remember occurs because Taro paid attention to the message of being undeserving and therefore gave energy up to an archetype in the collective unconscious. He then lacked the necessary ego energy to adhere to the words of his bride. Only by the vigilant attention of a tenacious ego, and a heroic effort of will, can we hope to emerge and remain in the unbounded, life energy realm of the psychoid—Taro's magnificent palace.

For consciousness to emerge into such unrestricted existence, it must overcome both creation's boundary and the gods' script. These barriers represent both the gods' sense of us and our own acceptance of that sense. The gods' (archetypes') fear of our freedom and our own fear of freedom reinforces the foundations of our barriers. To break through is a formidable challenge for the ego and may, at the moment, seem impossible to you. In fact, if life energy were contained only within the boundaried world and restricted by it, our challenge would be hopeless. Fortunately, we have the opportunity to evolve because the original life energy substance still exists beyond these confines. It turns out that my childhood night visitor is from this infinite beyond and has had much to do with my birth into a new life, into a psychoidal life.

Chapter 2

A MYTH OF DIVINE HEALING

EVEN THOUGH JUNG BASED his theory of the psyche on a closed energy system, he did realize that the individuation process, which was his solution to full maturity and harmony within the psyche, was only a first step along an individual's path of development.[1] As it turns out, my pursuit to understand the mystery of my ethereal night visitor led me beyond Jung's "first step" and onto a very unexpected, new path: a path that takes mature consciousness beyond the psyche into relationship with the psychoid and, in particular, into relationship with the ally, my ethereal visitor. The ally comes from the psychoid to act as catalyst and midwife to our evolution. My night visitor certainly catalyzed my growth, simply by its powerful, unexpected presence, which left an indelible mark in my memory. Several of the people who work with me have had similar catalyzing experiences, in which the ally accelerates individuation by relentlessly pushing one beyond Jung's first step. At the same time, the ally becomes midwife to our birth into the psychoid by pulling us toward it.

The process of liberation evolves through a series of transformations involving both God and humans. As Jung described, the first step of individuation accomplishes the formation of an ego-Self relationship to create a manifest Self that is a consciousness of truly knowing who one is. In other words, one's uniqueness is realized.

In this first step, humans and God must each create a manifest Self. In the second step, God's manifest Self and a person's manifest Self unite to produce a newly expanded, shared consciousness, which we have named the *latent* Psychoid Self. As stated in chapter I, and as we will confirm later, in the Juglan myth, there is a "third other" life form that exists outside of us and God. The third step of liberating consciousness requires this third other life form to be joined in the union of God and humans. The third transformation of consciousness then occurs, resulting in creation of the *manifest* Psychoid Self. Thus consciousness evolves through a series of Self transformations beyond all previously acknowledged boundaries into the realm of unlimited life energy.

The Myth of Juglan

My ally, in a series of meditations, presented a new mythology to me— the myth of Juglan—which illustrates this process. This creation myth contains several new ideas, and provides the hope and the means for our ego-Self to continue individuating beyond the psyche into unlimited resources of life energy, thereby liberating us from the cyclical pattern of life and death. I have left the words intact, just as they were given to me, in spite of their awkwardness. Although the name "Memory" can cause confusion, since it refers to our concept of ally, it works in this myth because it is directly associated with consciousness and that is exactly what the myth is about: the evolution of consciousness. "Ally" has an endearing quality and is appropriately used to relate to the work of personal psychoidal individuation. In the discussion following the myth, I use the term "Memory/ally" to identify this duality. The myth, as it was given to me, follows:

In the beginning was Juglan. Juglan sat alone in darkness, in a "non-state." There was neither consciousness nor unconsciousness. When this non-state could be no more, a splitting sound ripped Juglan in half. Evolution began.

Each half became lost from the other. One was called Spirare, clothed in the god. The other was called Saiwala, clothed in the human. Spirare and Saiwala sensed a separation and loss of wholeness. They felt themselves to be wounded, and this was the first Knowing.

Creation began as Spirare and Saiwala attempted to cleanse their wounds. Separate worlds formed, each in the shadow of the other. Unknown to each other, Saiwala's and Spirare's threads of compensation wove themselves each into a separate blanket, soothing their pain of incompleteness, yet obscuring the Truth of the other. They became wrapped in alienation and loneliness. The inhabitants of these two worlds lived bound by their respective illusions of being whole unto themselves and thus remained ignorant of the other.

Now, in the initial splitting, a third other was born. It was called Memory. Memory knew the Truth. Spoken in dreams, Truth leaked through the blanket. These dreams sought out ready recipients of each world, drawing them toward Memory. Those whose focus held tight to Memory saw the Truth of the other. In seeing they exclaimed, "We are found to each other, equal, now whole. I am Juglan Illuminated." This exclamation was brief, as Spirare, Saiwala, and Memory became the one Luminous Tree, EO, meant to be. This was the greatest Knowing.

~

This story, similar to most creation myths, begins with the pregnant potential of creation, as represented by Juglan. Juglan, which is the scientific name for walnut, is a two-lobed seed that, when removed from its shell, appears to have two equal halves. If this seed remains intact, a tree will eventually grow from it. Instead, in the Juglan myth, the seed splits into three parts. This three-part splitting is significant because a new thing, a thing that differs from the two lobes, has been added for the future development of creation. Memory/ally, which is a third "half," will provide an entirely new dimension to the original two-lobed seed.

The seed, now pregnant with itself, seethes with potential life energy. If it were to remain intact and follow the course of nature, a tree would grow; the seed is actually locked into the "script of tree." As I mentioned in the previous chapter, there is usually a reason for the way in which mythical creation occurs. In traditional myths, a womb is created to house the development of human consciousness. In this story, the splitting creates two wombs: one for God and one for humans, so that each can develop its own manifest Self. The splitting causes a disruption in nature's script, by creating a third element that opens the possibility of an entirely new result. The dynamics of evolution demand that nature be opened to change. Remember that it is the opening of our closed system that allows for our birth into a new life, so that Juglan's splitting into three parts allows for an entirely new outcome (other than the tree) to occur. The possibility for the third step of Self transformation has now been set up. Memory/ally, Juglan's third part, will realign the course of nature or catalyze evolution. This possibility exists only because Memory/ally was created, since Memory/ally is entirely separate from the twin lobes, Spirare and Saiwala.

Now these twin lobes that are split apart represent the more familiar world of humans and God. The half named Spirare, which, in Latin,
is related to "spirit," is the residence of the god(s). The fact that the
gods have their own, closed, separate world parallels many of the myths
in which divine realms are described as both separate from humans and
within the confines of an enclosed world. In the Babylonian myth,
Marduk constructs a dwelling place under the vault; in Genesis (1:1-8),
God's heaven is in the vault; and in the Gnostic story, the gods reside
beneath a dividing veil. Who the gods assume themselves to be, along
with what humans project onto them, forms the veil of illusions or, in
this story, the woven blanket that keeps gods and humans separated.
Likewise, people's assumption of who they are, along with what the
gods project onto them, forms yet another dividing blanket. These separate worlds act as wombs for the respective maturation of both God's
and human's consciousness to give each the ability to truly see the other.
This is the first step toward liberation. Formation of both these manifest Selves allows the blanket to unravel.

A Dual Individuation

It really is not unusual in myths or stories to see God and humans living in separate realms. What is unusual is to imagine God's world as
reflective of God's psyche just as the human world symbolically represents the human psyche. The Juglan myth describes both the human
psyche and God's psyche as being incomplete and in need of healing.
If there is ever going to be a tree, the two halves must come back into
union, which is the second stage of Self transformation. For this to
take place, both halves must become fully conscious and, because

Jung's individuation process is about realizing one's unique wholeness, individuation applies to both humans (Saiwala) and God (Spirare). The individuation process, in which one works on truly knowing oneself, will eventually unravel the "blanket" that obscures both people's and God's vision. This first step of transformation (dual individuation) is critical for the assurance of an eventual union between God and human.

The ally is instrumental in this process in the same way that it is instrumental in human individuation; by coming into dreams, meditations or real life experiences. Memory/ally holds the blueprint of wholeness and knows what both God and people are capable of becoming. So while an individual individuates or creates a mature consciousness centered on the ego-Self, God also individuates by creating a consciousness centered on its ego-Self. As will be described below, based on the twin nature of God's psyche (Spirare) and the human psyche (Saiwala) their centers are mirror opposites. This invert nature aids Memory/ally in its task of bringing these centers into union, since it is as if the two are moving into themselves.

Ironically then, God's Self is symbolized by the "human" image and we will soon see how man's Self is symbolized by the "God" image. There are numerous references in other creation myths to humans being made in the image of a creator, such as the Eskimo creator Raven, who throws off his disguise and reveals himself to be human. In *Jung's Last Years*, Jaffé quotes Jung, "Man is the mirror which God holds up before him, or the sense organ with which he apprehends his being."[2] Thus, the symbolic image for Spirare's center is human and represents God's manifest Self, which we are naming the "God-Divine" center.[3]

The other half of Juglan's two-lobed seed is Saiwala, which in Gothic means "soul." This human sphere correlates to the human psyche, which Jung spent a lifetime describing. He concluded from his work, particularly in alchemy, that the God image symbolized the self.[4] In most, the divine maker adds some element of itself to the human composition. Therefore, each human contains divineness, which the Juglan myth describes as Saiwala's Self. This Self that is considered to be the human manifest Self we are naming as the "human-Divine" center.[5] It is distinct from the God-Divine center, just as identical twins are distinct yet equal.

So both God and humans contain their reflective, respective divine centers, transformed through individuation from latent states into manifest Selves. In the Juglan myth, both Selves originate from the same source: Juglan, the original life energy. Thus, God and humans, independently, attain their respective Divine centers (their Selves) from Juglan, which remain latent until each individuates. This idea differs from the traditional notion of a human's divinity being dependent upon God giving the divinity to human beings. In this new philosophy, the psychic structures of God and humans are mirror images, or twins. Spirare (God's psyche) and Saiwala (the human psyche), being equal in content, have equal need of each other in order to fulfill the possibility of becoming whole (the tree). This possibility for wholeness occurs when a person sees himself or herself in God and God sees Itself in the person. This act of "seeing" happens through the symbolism of the human Self and God's Self. God and humans are able to enter into union when they realize this truth and are then able to create the latent Psychoid Self. In this state, the consciousnesses of both God and the person have broken out of their closed realms and into the psychoid.

Without the union of Spirare and Saiwala, they each remain unfulfilled, incapable of becoming what they can be.

The idea of God (Spirare) being incomplete may seem incomprehensible. Since God's Self is symbolized by the human, then consider the possibility that God's becoming incarnate as human is its attempt to acquire knowledge of its Self and hence, make manifest its God-Divine center. Meanwhile, people so often strive to become perfect; this could be thought of as their incarnation as God. Such striving arises from our projection of perfection onto God. Support for both these premises comes from a collective heritage that includes both the Egyptian account of the journey human souls take to become God and the Christian teaching in which God becomes man. Through this mutual awareness of the other and acquisition of Divine centers, both God and humans realize their twin natures so that feelings of alienation from one another dissolve. The Hindu philosophy of Śivaism, which destroys illusions,[6] supports this idea, particularly in Kriṣna's response to Śiva: "for we are not distinct one from the other: what thou art that I am also."[7]

Reunion of the Halves, The Divine-Divine Center

Such recognition by God and humans opens the way for a union of the seed of Juglan, so that a tree might evolve. The two halves actually need each to make the tree happen. This shared bit of wisdom allows God and humans to enter into a mutually respectful relationship, one which requires consciousness of "I" and "other." Therefore, the ego of both God and humans must stay intact so that neither loses consciousness: People take their "humanness" into the relationship of Saiwala (human psyche) and Spirare (God's psyche) in the same way that God takes his "godness" into the relationship. Consequently, neither humans nor God are devalued, and the new, shared union that follows creates yet a new center, the latent Psychoid Self. We are naming this the "Divine-Divine" center.[8] It offers the possibility for a third Self transformation and creation of another entirely new center that can be compared to the production of electricity by combining the waterwheel (human) with water (God) or to the nature of light as both particle (human) and wave (God). God and humans will thus be rewarded for their union. Their simultaneous transformation will create something entirely wonderful and different from each other.

But this new center of consciousness, the Divine-Divine center, would shift back onto nature's scripted path were it not for Memory/ally. Understanding the nature of the Divine-Divine center is rather complicated. The Psychoid Self is the center of the Divine, as referred to in chapter I. (Remember that the Divine is the unrestricted, unbounded realm that includes both the created and the yet-to-be created.) Memory/ally, the third other created in the Juglan myth, must be included in the Divine-Divine center, for it is only through this inclusion that the Psychoid Self becomes manifest. The Juglan myth names the manifest Psychoid Self as EO or the Luminous Tree.[9]

Transformation of the Divine-Divine

Paradoxically, the manifested Psychoid Self, or EO, is the embodied Memory/ally. The "knowledge of what was and what is to be" is an attribute of the Self. Memory/ally has possessed this knowledge and, therefore, is a prefiguration of EO, the Luminous Tree. It begins as a prefiguration but through the successive Self transformations, Memory/ally culminates as the Luminous Tree. It is as if Memory/ally is the center of the Divine in the making. And, the making of this center requires the relationship of humans and God with the ally. This relationship then leads to the union of the person and God, which forms the Divine-Divine center. This formation must occur prior to the manifestation of the Luminous Tree. Thus, we are actually co-creators in this endeavor.

After Memory/ally orchestrates the formation of the Divine-Divine center, it completes the transformation into the Luminous Tree by becoming part of the union. Thus, in terms of the Juglan myth, the third element (Memory/ally) that came into being when Juglan split is now included in the restored seed, and the course of nature's closed script has been altered.

Memory/ally works toward its own manifestation by constructing a path and guiding us on it to create the human-Divine center, the God-Divine center, and the Divine-Divine center. Memory/ally has the advantage of being outside the two realms so that it can provide missing knowledge for both God and people. It provides this knowledge to both by sending images, visions and big life experiences that evoke strong feeling reactions. Through these attention-grabbers, Memory/ally pulls the focus of both toward a relationship with it to catalyze their individuation and ultimately transform God, humans, and the ally into the Luminous Tree.

A relationship with Memory/ally catalyzes formation of the Divine centers (Selves). Through this relationship, Memory/ally includes itself in the individuation processes of the person's and God's manifest Selves. Because Memory/ally is included when these centers join to become the Divine-Divine center, the existence of this center is very brief. Triggered instantly by Memory/ally's intention to complete the process, all are then transfigured in this final transformation into EO, the Luminous Tree.

The Luminous Tree, EO

This tree is not just the original, ordinary tree of Juglan. Now it is Luminous, in the greatest Knowing. EO radiates with eternal iridescence because it has broken free of the cyclical pattern of death and regeneration. The tree is Luminous because it is lit by the transfigured consciousness of the human, God and the ally that will sustain its ability to infinitely evolve. Consciousness, because of its series of "Self" transformations, moves into the realm of unlimited life energy. The tree has its roots in Earth and branches in Heaven or vice versa; it represents the ordinary tree grown from Juglan. However, EO, the Luminous Tree, is derived from the union of Juglan and Memory/ally and has surpassed that ordinary tree which merely grows "into that which eternally is and does not change."[10] EO, the Luminous Tree, eternally changes. Its roots are unbound. The Luminous Tree has the capacity for limitless and unimaginable possibilities.

A person becomes this Luminous Tree by sharing union with God and Memory/ally. But why would a person want to evolve to such consciousness? Quite simply, a person gains conscious immortality by consciously participating in the evolution of his or her Self, God, and Memory/ally. Therefore, there is never risk of a static existence. The person gains a shared intimacy with the Divine, which eliminates fear and loneliness. The person becomes rooted in the very essence or sap of Life, itself, and receives a tremendous sense of belonging. This is the dawning of our new existence.

Chapter 3

THE STAGES OF
DIVINE TRANSFORMATION

THE JUGLAN MYTH provides a design for our evolution beyond a closed existence. This design entails successive stages of Self development that culminate in the achievement of a new psychoid existence. The following three tales will be used to help amplify the evolutionary stages of the myth: the Native American story called "Jumping Mouse"[1] deals with the interactive transformations of Saiwala (the human psyche) and Spirare (God's psyche) and, especially, with the manifestation of the human-Divine center; the African tale of "The Hero Makoma"[2] describes the process of evolving into the psychoid via creation of the Divine-Divine center; the third story is my own, titled, "Broken Eggs." It describes the final stage of transformation into EO, the Luminous Tree.

Although "Memory" is the original name from the Juglan myth, for our concept of the ally I am now dropping the "Memory" from Memory/ally in favor of the more personal name of "ally." Because of the familiarity and intimacy that evolves between Memory/ally and the individual who takes this path, the name "ally" better suits the feel of the personal relationship that develops. Therefore, the term "ally" will be used throughout the rest of the book.

Jumping Mouse

A very busy, small Mouse, with his whiskers to the ground, one day hears a very odd sound and lifts his head in wonder. He asks the other mice if they, too, hear a roaring in their ears. Being very busy with their mouse work, they say, "We hear nothing," and they scold small Mouse for his questions. Embarrassed, small Mouse returns to his work. However, the roaring in his ears continues to distract him, so small Mouse relents and goes to investigate.

With great fear, he leaves the mouse community and moves in the direction of the sound. Soon, someone shouts, "Hello!" Raccoon introduces himself and asks what Mouse is doing all alone. The small Mouse answers, "I keep hearing a roar in my ears and am following the sound."

Raccoon identifies the roar as the sound of the River, and asks, "Do you want me to take you there?" Despite Mouse's fear, he allows Raccoon to lead him to the River. Along the way, the small Mouse encounters several new smells that increase his fear, but he does not turn back.

The River they reach is so huge that Mouse cannot see the other side. Raccoon now introduces Mouse to Frog and then bids him farewell. Frog says to Mouse, "I am Keeper of the Water and I can offer you some medicine power. Are you interested?"

Very curious, Mouse responds, "Yes!"

So Frog whispers, "Crouch as low as you can and then jump as high as you are able. You will have your medicine." The small Mouse does as instructed and at the height of his jump he sees the Sacred Mountains. He can hardly believe the sight. But then, the small Mouse falls and lands in the River. Wet and frightened he scrambles up to shore. Frog gives Mouse a new name, proclaiming, "Your name is now Jumping Mouse!"

Jumping Mouse runs excitedly back to the community of mice and tells them of his vision of the Sacred Mountains. No one listens. In fact, they are afraid of the soaking wet Jumping Mouse, because there has been no rain, they know of no River and, therefore, they have no explanation for his wetness. Jumping Mouse attempts to return to the life of his mouse community, but cannot forget his vision.

One day, as Jumping Mouse looks across the land from the edge of his community, the urge to go to the Sacred Mountains wins out over his fear of being ridiculed. Jumping Mouse has something else to fear: the sky fills with the shadow of an eagle. He gathers up courage and, with a pounding heart, Jumping Mouse runs across the land. He scurries into a stand of sage, haven for mice and the home of Old Mouse, who says that you can see all on the land and know their names. When Jumping Mouse asks him about the River and the Sacred Mountains, Old Mouse responds, "Yes, I know about the River, but the Sacred Mountains are only a myth. Forget about your vision and stay with me." Jumping Mouse is horrified, as the vision of the Mountains cannot be forgotten. He continues his quest.

It is hard to leave; however, once again, Jumping Mouse musters up the determination and courage and runs across the land, feeling the shadow of an eagle on his back. He scurries into a stand of chokecherries where it is cool, spacious, full of water, and all things to eat. While investigating, Jumping Mouse hears the heavy breathing of Great Buffalo. Great Buffalo greets Jumping Mouse and Jumping Mouse asks, "Why are you lying upon the ground?"

Great Buffalo sighs, "I am dying and can only be healed by the eye of a mouse, which does not exist."

Jumping Mouse sits fretting with this realization and soon decides that Great Buffalo must not die. He returns to Great Buffalo's side, "I am a mouse and you may have my eye." The eye flies out of Jumping Mouse and into Great Buffalo, who becomes whole. Great Buffalo thanks Jumping Mouse and, knowing of Jumping

Mouse's quest, offers him protection beneath his belly. In this way, they cross the land, easing Jumping Mouse's fear of the shadow.

Great Buffalo takes Jumping Mouse to the base of the Sacred Mountains and bids him farewell. Jumping Mouse once again begins to explore, discovering more here than at any of the other places. He also discovers a quiet, gray wolf. Jumping Mouse approaches, saying, "Hello, Wolf."

Wolf suddenly becomes alert and exclaims, "Wolf! That is what I am!" And then he is quiet again. Jumping Mouse realizes that Wolf has no memory and sits quietly with this knowledge. Finally, Jumping Mouse makes up his mind to help Wolf. "I know what you need," he tells Wolf. "You may have my other eye."

The eye flies out of Jumping Mouse, healing Wolf. Now, Wolf is whole, but Jumping Mouse is blind. Wolf reveals himself, "I am the guide into the Sacred Mountains, where there is a great Medicine Lake in which the entire world is reflected. I can take you there." Wolf takes Jumping Mouse to the Lake on top of the Sacred Mountains and then returns to his post at the base of the mountains.

Jumping Mouse trembles with fear at being left alone again, knowing the nearness of the eagle's shadow. Feeling eagle's closeness, he braces for its hit. Jumping Mouse falls unconscious. When he wakes, Jumping Mouse is not only alive, but is also able to see. As he jumps about in excitement, he hears a familiar voice, "Do you want some medicine? Crouch as low as you can and jump as high as you can."

Jumping Mouse does as told. The wind catches Jumping Mouse and carries him higher and higher. The voice calls, "Don't be afraid, hang on to the wind and trust. You have a new name. You are Eagle."

~

This story amplifies the process of individuation within the human psyche. It is a powerful tale of trust and sacrifice in order to achieve one's human-Divine center. Jung defined individuation as consciousness that separates from the collective path in order to cut a new path.[3] For Jumping Mouse, the new path culminates with the formation of a symbolic human-Divine center as Eagle. Mouse's transformations, as he separates from his mice world (the collective path), occur because he trusts in his senses and adheres to the memory of his experiences. Following the roar in his ears, Mouse becomes Jumping Mouse. And, Jumping Mouse's relentless memory of his river experience and vision of the Sacred Mountains becomes the catalyst for his eventual transformation into Eagle. Mouse's memory of his eye's healing power restores Wolf's memory and this enables Mouse to achieve his final transformation into Eagle. In like manner, the relentless memory of powerful experiences and the trust in these experiences lead many individuals onto the path of individuation, which transforms consciousness.

A new Self consciousness is exactly what Jumping Mouse obtains when he becomes Eagle. In Carlos Castaneda's *The Eagle's Gift*, the eagle as a power that governs destiny gives its gift of power in order to keep the "flame of awareness" alive.[4] Awareness is directly related to both memory and consciousness. It is dependent upon memory to maintain awareness and, as a field, it defines one's consciousness. Memory, like the ally, maintains Jumping Mouse's awareness and thus directs his focus. He then achieves a transformed consciousness that represents the human-Divine center. This center gives Mouse a new dimension and the vision to see beyond his boundary into God's psyche.

The vital role that memory (ally) plays in keeping awareness alive for the benefit of consciousness is also talked about in Plato's myth of Er:[5]

A soldier named Er, who dies in battle, arises on the twelfth day, just as his family is about to bury him. Restored, he begins to tell the story of a soul's journey that he witnessed while dead. All the souls are first directed to either heaven or hell. They then return from their respective places and go to a meadow. Here, they mingle with each other and share experiences. On the eighth day, all of the souls journey to the Pillar of Light and there encounter the three Fates. Each soul picks up the lot next to them, which is thrown to the souls by one of the Fates. The souls are told that since they pick up their own lot that is their fate, God is to be blameless for their fate. With their destinies sealed, the souls march into the Plain of Forgetfulness and drink from the River of Indifference so that they forget everything, becoming ignorant. Er explains, "I am spared from death to tell you not to drink from the river, so that you won't return to the world ignorant."

~

In this story, Er comes back to life in order to persuade us to avoid what he witnessed: the march through the "Plain of Forgetfulness" and the "River of Indifference." If the listener's soul retains the memory of Er's story, it can avoid the "march" into ignorance and instead, preserve consciousness. The preserved consciousness will not return ignorant to the body and can, therefore, hope to evolve beyond the closed world.

Let's return to the Jumping Mouse story and its images of Eagle, River and Medicine Lake. Cirlot, in his *Dictionary of Symbols*, states that the eagle in Egyptian hieroglyphs symbolizes origin and life's essence.[6] Recall our Juglan myth where origin refers to the united seed. The same theme, that of moving toward the origin or seed of life, is expressed in Jumping Mouse through the images of the River and Medicine Lake. River's origin, which is the Lake atop the Sacred

Mountains, contains the entire world or "all of life." In mythology, water is often synonymous with the origin of life. Jumping Mouse's River experience ignites his passion and draws him to this lake of origin. It is as if life itself seeks transformation; Jumping Mouse's adherence to the memory of his River experience fuels his individuation journey. Medicine Lake, the "Origin" that creates the River, draws Mouse to it through Eagle.

The Eagle symbolizes destiny. Jumping Mouse's constant avoidance of Eagle's shadow illustrates his unconscious fear of destiny. So, as long as he fearfully avoids Eagle, Mouse is ignorant of his potential destiny. The Eagle's shadow portends Mouse's future. Mouse is driven by his own fear of the Eagle into becoming the Eagle, which is actually Mouse's true manifest identity. In my practice, I have often seen people fear their latent Selves while, simultaneously, they feel pushed toward manifesting that Self. So the ego dances about trying to avoid its partner, the Self, until the critical moment when ego and Self connect and the human-Divine center manifests. I want to emphasize that the ego is of critical importance because the Self isn't manifest until the ego comes into relationship with it.

In our story, this moment of connection occurs immediately following the instructions given to Mouse by Frog. Frog, an animal of metamorphosis, is the voice of the ally, who coaxes Jumping Mouse into his transfiguration. Jumping Mouse does not return to his origin: he does not fall into the Lake, which symbolizes unconsciousness. Instead, as Eagle, he rises into a new dimension that carries him beyond the Lake.

This is incredibly significant. By not falling into the Lake, Mouse/Eagle maintains consciousness and his identity. With his intact human-Divine center, Jumping Mouse is able to evolve beyond the human psyche. As his existence changes in dimension from ground to sky and in form from mouse to eagle, he comes into his supra-ordinate being: his human-Divine center.

These changes have occurred only because Mouse has consciously departed from one system after another: first from the mice, then from Old Mouse, Buffalo, Wolf and, finally, from the Lake and ground. The mice world from which Mouse escapes represents instinctual, automated behavior and thought. This is a life of unconsciousness where one simply follows and imitates a collectively set pattern of being. Jumping Mouse extricates himself from this unconscious state of existence and encounters Old Mouse, who attempts to trap the former with the lure of comfort in the stand of sage, and power, which comes from the act of naming. (Traditionally, to know a name is to have power over that which is named.) These temptations compare to complexes that tend to derail a person from becoming who he or she is. The complex appeals to the ego's weakness, in this case, that it needs or wants comfort or power. The complex also casts doubt on the ego's experiences in the same way that Old Mouse tries to dismiss Mouse's "seeing" of the Sacred Mountains. Every time we dismiss one of our personal experiences as "not real," we succumb to Old Mouse's influence. If we become caught up by this influence (complexes), we will become stranded in the sage and our journey toward transformation will end there. Fortunately, Jumping Mouse avoids the trap and continues on, encountering the guides, Buffalo and Wolf. These two animals symbolize the Spirit and thus represent the latent Self. Jumping Mouse is able to hear and respond to each Spirit's need of healing, so that, by his sacrificial response, he can complete the manifestation of his human-Divine center.

Mouse's departures from the mice world, Old Mouse, Buffalo, and Wolf represent successive disentanglement from a closed world. Mouse's achievement of each departure requires his constant focus on his goal of unraveling the mystery of the sound in his ears and then the mystery of the Sacred Mountains. Jumping Mouse maintains his focus by trusting in his experiences and then acting upon them, despite collective ridicule or personal fear. Trust in ourselves is the most essential element for growth, yet, trust is the most difficult asset to come by. People, too, have been thoroughly brainwashed by the collective "mice mentality" and "Old Mouse's complexes" until they do not believe their own personal experiences.

I found it extremely difficult to learn to trust my inner messages, especially when they were pushing me to go against my ego's desires. Several years ago, dream sequences and meditations directed me to leave the Interregional Jungian Training program so I could pursue my intuitions about the psychoid. But, after investing nearly four years in the Jungian training program, I wanted my certification and the societal recognition and power that accompanied it. I also wanted to "belong" to a group. An intense inner conflict arose. As a result, I resisted the guidance of those dreams and meditations and chose not to trust my ally's messages. What a mistake! One morning I arrived at my office to find it soaking wet. An analyst, who shared an office near mine, informed me that my radiator had broken and the steam had built up in my office, threatening to cause an explosion. To excuse the incident as coincidence was impossible, since everything in my office was destroyed by the steam, except for one Kachina, made of wood, feathers, and leather, which was the Kachina of my ally.[7] It sat directly above the radiator, yet was untouched and dry. That night I composed my letter of resignation to the Interregional Jungian Training program.

Unlike most people, Jumping Mouse demonstrates heroic trust in his uncomplicated evasion of the mice and Old Mouse. Jumping Mouse has tremendous guts and sheer willpower. His inherent traits sustain his individuation because he has an ego that is capable of staying focused. Jumping Mouse can overcome his fear of death that comes from Eagle's shadow, and thereby cross each boundary. The fear of death when crossing a boundary is a common feeling experience shared by most of the people with whom I have worked. This is a fear of both physical death and psychic death, which would be the loss of one's sense of identity or ego. The fear of death seems to be built into the very fabric of a closed system in order to discourage transgressors, so it takes great courage and concentration to accomplish the journey of individuation.

Perhaps Jumping Mouse's greatest act of trust and courage is in the sacrifice of his eyes to Buffalo and Wolf. He accepts that each of these Spirits needs healing, and that it can only come from the gift of an eye. The eye's significance lies in its multifaceted symbolism. Loss of an eye causes increased darkness that is associated with the act of reflection. We turn inward by closing our eyes in order to discover the Self, lying hidden in the darkness. "Rare is he who . . . shuts his eyes to what is without and beholds the Self."[8] Jumping Mouse becomes this rare person when he gives up his outer sight.

The act of reflection also allows one to perceive differently.

Jumping Mouse's act shows his willingness to "let go" of his way of see-ing, or way of perception. This heroic act of trust in letting go of one's set of beliefs and ideas is essential in the process of individuation.

Such an act allows for the subsequent relationship between Mouse, Buffalo, and Wolf to occur. This relationship is analogous to the estab-lishment of an ego-Self relationship. The play on the words "eye" and "I" suggests this psychological parallel: "I" represents the ego while the Spirits (Buffalo and Wolf) represent the latent Self. This relationship becomes mutually beneficial in that Buffalo and Wolf are restored to wholeness, helping Jumping Mouse to realize his full potential. Similarly, the Egyptian soul (Ba) returns with consciousness to the spirit light (Akh), thus changing Akh with its knowledge.[9]

When Jumping Mouse sacrifices his eye (I), he actually forsakes his ego-centered attitude. This opens him to the connection with the spirit or, psychologically, to an ego-Self relationship. This relationship becomes the human-Divine center. The ego-centered attitude is difficult to surrender since we are traditionally schooled to believe in our own human neediness and to seek out God's intervention to correct our cir-cumstances. Rarely do people consider God to be in dire neediness. I was given a shocking view of this neediness during a visionary experi-ence. Transported into the psychoid, I saw a cave full of allies, who were chained to the walls and starving for freedom. I "knew," in that moment, their need for our attention and relation.

Jumping Mouse responds to these needs by paying attention to his experiences, trusting himself, staying focused and, despite fear, following the ally beyond the known into the unknown. The ally hopefully affects our heart, in the way it did for Jumping Mouse, so that we might respond to the call of evolution to eventually become EO, the Luminous Tree. Jumping Mouse completes the first step of individuation by establishing a human-Divine center that exists within his psyche, symbolized by the transformation into Eagle.

The stage is now set for going beyond Jung's first step in individuation. The second step would be the union of the human-Divine center with the God-Divine center, which is described in the African tale "The Hero Makoma."

The Hero Makoma

In a small village, a most unusual child is born with a large sack in one hand, an iron hammer in the other, and the speech of a grown man. One day his mother asks, "By what name do you want to be called?"

The child instructs his mother to gather all the village leaders to the deep black pool in the river where the crocodiles live. When they have all gathered about the pool, the child challenges the leaders to leap into it and overcome the crocodiles. No one responds. Suddenly, the child dives into the dark pool and disappears.

All of those gathered gasp at what the child has done, "Surely, he must be crazy! He has just thrown his life away to the crocodiles!"

Then the ground begins to tremble and the pool turns red with blood. The child surfaces, no longer a child, but a strong, handsome man. The leaders cheer as the man announces his name, "I am Makoma, the Greater."

Makoma tells his mother that he must make a home of his own and become a hero. He departs with his iron hammer and sack. Makoma wanders for many days, until one day, he meets a huge giant who is building mountains.

Makoma shouts a greeting and asks, "Who are you?"

He replies, "I am the Maker of Mountains and who are you?"

Makoma shouts back, "I am Makoma the Greater, greater than you!"

The giant gives a roar and attacks. Makoma swings his hammer, hitting the giant on the head so hard that the giant shrinks into a small man. The giant exclaims, "You are great! Please, take me with you." So Makoma puts the giant into his sack and, having acquired the giant's strength, resumes his journey.

Soon he crosses the path of another giant who is pulling up huge chunks of earth. Makoma asks, "Who are you?"

The giant replies, "I am Maker of Riverbeds. Who are you?"

Makoma shouts his name, "I am Makoma the Greater!"

With that, the giant attacks him. Makoma rushes in with his hammer, striking the giant so hard that he, too, becomes quite small. Makoma tosses him into his sack.

He continues on his way, now filled with this giant's power. Soon he comes across yet another giant who is planting trees and cries out, "Who are you?"

"I am Planter of Trees. Who are you?" responds the giant.

"I am Makoma the Greater!" challenges Makoma.

The giant attacks. With the iron hammer, Makoma shrinks this giant into a small man. He, too, is placed in the sack.

Filled with this giant's power, Makoma travels on for many days until he sees a giant eating fire. Makoma demands, "Who are you?"

This giant laughs, "I am the Flame Spirit and can destroy anything."

"Well, you can't destroy me, because I am Makoma the Great!"

Laughing, the Flame Spirit attacks Makoma. Makoma jumps aside and throws his iron hammer, hitting the giant, who shrinks into a small man. Again, he adds this giant to his sack. Now, he is truly a great hero.

Wandering on, Makoma comes across a great plain in the middle of which is a green meadow with all the food and water he could want. Stopping here, he takes all the giants out of his sack, saying, "My friends, lets make this home!"

And so, each day Makoma and the giants go out to collect what is necessary for constructing a home, leaving one giant to tend the camp. However, each time they return to camp, the giant that tends the camp is rendered helpless by a "man out of the river," who always comes exactly at high noon. Frustrated, Makoma states, "I am staying to see just who this is that renders my friends helpless."

The giants then leave him at camp. And just as foretold, when the sun is directly overhead at midday, Makoma hears a rumbling from the river. He watches as an enormous man emerges, whose moustache spreads up and down the riverbed as far as can be seen. The giant shouts, "Who are you?"

Makoma gives his name and says, "Before I kill you, tell me who you are!"

"I am the Fever Spirit and I bring death to all who come to me."

"You won't do that to me!" challenges Makoma.

A battle begins that forces Makoma to use more than just his hammer. The Fever Spirit is so slippery that Makoma must throw his sack over the giant's head to keep his hammer from slipping. This time the giant is killed.

When the four giants return to camp, they celebrate Makoma's feat. Unfortunately, when they awake the following morning, Makoma tells them of a foreboding dream. "My friends, last night I was visited by the spirits of my fathers, who told me that I must journey alone to find the five-headed being, Sakatirini. So I must say goodbye to you." Makoma returns to each saddened giant their strengths and gifts.

He spends the next several days traveling until he reaches a hut near some large peaks. He greets the women of the hut, asking, "Do you know of Sakatirini, and where I can find him?"

They all respond at once, "You have found him! You are standing at his feet. Those tall mountain peaks are the legs of Sakatirini, but the rest of him is hidden in the clouds."

Makoma strides forward and, with his hammer, strikes the feet of Sakatirini several times until he finally responds, "Who scratches my feet?"

"I, Makoma the Greater!"

There is no answer, so Makoma builds a fire at Sakatirini's feet. "Who makes a fire burn at my feet?"

"I, Makoma. I have been sent by the spirits of my ancestors to find you so that I won't grow weary of myself."

Sakatirini sighs, "I am also growing weary. I am all alone because no man is as great as I."

Sakatirini then reaches down and grabs Makoma, dashing him to the ground. Surprisingly, Makoma doesn't die, but instead, becomes full of life and equal in size to Sakatirini. They enter into a great wrestling match that neither can win. After several hours, they fall exhausted onto the ground, wrapped in each others arms. When they awake, the Great Spirit from Beyond greets them: "You have become such great heroes that no one may come against you. I am taking you from the world to live with me." And, as the Great Spirit speaks, they leave the world as equals for their new home beyond the clouds.

~

We know immediately from this story that Makoma has the mark of a hero. He has unusual attributes of speech and strength at birth and he comes into the world with a hammer in his hand. In myths, a hammer is directly related to the gods: both P'an Ku from a Chinese creation myth, and Thor, a Norse god, have hammers that they use to forge the world.[10] The root word for "forge" comes from the Indo-European word *dhabh*, which means "to join or fit." Makoma's destiny of joining himself to Sakatirini is thus foretold. This joining is analogous to the union of the human-Divine center and the God-Divine center that creates the Divine-Divine center. Makoma is forging a new consciousness similar to the Gods' forging of a new world. For individuals, as for Makoma, it requires heroic effort to extricate oneself from Saiwala (the human psyche).

Those people currently working to extricate themselves from the boundary of the human psyche toward union with the God-Divine center can certainly attest to the heroic strength this takes. One must stay focused on the goal, stay true to onself, and willingly depart from the comfort of familiarity and journey into the unknown.

People are "marked" by compelling dreams, visions or experiences that push them into the process of expanding consciousness just as Makoma and Jumping Mouse were when they responded to the quests of individuation. Makoma is "marked" and feels compelled to leave his home. Jumping Mouse also seemed to be born with a roar in his ears and an unquenchable need for understanding.

So the first step of individuation involves the formation of the human-Divine center through the establishment of an ego-Self relationship. Makoma accomplishes this step at the beginning of the story when he dives into, and exits out of, the pool. This scene might remind one of a baptism in which either water or blood are the medium. Makoma's initiation into successive stages of his development is symbolized by his descent into the dark pool. This is his descent into the unconscious. A person's descent into the unconscious, via dream analysis, initiates the dreamer onto the path of individuation. Makoma's emergence from the "blood red pool" tells us that he conquered the crocodiles, guardians of the "treasure hard to attain." Here, the treasure hard to attain is the Self or one's true nature. Similarly, in Egyptian mythology, the soul's successful journey through the underworld brings it into "crocodile knowledge:" the knowledge of one's nature and destiny. So, Makoma's success against crocodiles earns him the new name of Makoma the Greater. As such, he has realized his human-Divine center.

There is additional significance to the symbol of blood in Makoma's pool. In the popular phrase "blood brothers," blood is recognized as a binding agent. Makoma becomes bound in blood to his newly acquired "human-Divine" center and its destiny. Makoma's honest adherence to his destiny eventually takes him beyond all illusory boundaries into an embrace with Sakatirini, the God-Divine center.

After Makoma emerges from the pool, he begins his exodus from the human psyche by leaving the familiarity of home, taking with him only his hammer and sack. We know from our previous look at hammer symbolism that a new world will be forged. Psychologically, this new world will be a new consciousness born beyond his human psyche. As Makoma approaches the boundary of his human psyche, he encounters four giants, which, according to Stewart in *The Elements of Creation Myth*, represent our original ancestors.[11] Marie-Louise Von Franz referred to giants as symbols of our raw psychic energy.[12] In this respect, we can think of Makoma's giants as original psychic or life energy. If you will remember from the Juglan myth, the original psychic energy was split in half. In that myth, Saiwala contained only half of the available energies. Spirare contained the other half. Makoma first collects human psychic energies in order to exit from the bounded world. He integrates that life energy every time he shrinks a giant with his hammer and places it into his sack. Active imagination is the psychological equivalent to this shrinking as it is a process of conscious dialogue with inner figures. In this way, one's human-Divine center accumulates energies, thus strengthening consciousness. In like manner, Makoma assimilates the power and attributes of the giants or obtains some of their original life energies each time he places one into his sack. His sack is a vessel for this energy transformation.

In order to add energy to the psyche and allow consciousness to grow, the psyche must be open. Here the number four becomes relevant. Four pillars are often used in creation mythology to hold up the sky vault that keeps the world closed. In the Icelandic creation myth, Ymir's skull is held up by four pillars, and in the Pawnee creation myth, four stars support the sky.[13] In the Navajo creation myth, reference is made to four mountains as support.[14] So, in Makoma's story, the four giants can be equated to the four pillars or supports used in other creation myths. These giants were instrumental to maintain a closed psyche, or woven blanket, or, in other words, a boundary. So when Makoma shrinks the giants, he has opened his psyche by bringing down the supports of the closed world. He thus unravels the blanket of illusions.

It is important to note that Makoma befriends the giants rather than destroying them, as they are representative of the psychic/life energies within his psyche. To destroy the giants would have meant destruction of raw psychic/life energies. Instead, Makoma comes into relationship with the giants. This allows him unlimited access to that original energy. When one participates in active imagination, one taps into the raw psychic energies of the inner figure. This connection is like being plugged into a main power plant and enables one to complete their journey.

Makoma releases the giants so they can return to their homes. His relationship with them is not one of bondage. Were he to hold on to them, if even in a friendly manner, Makoma would be repeating the fault of the closed world. At the time of the giants' release, Makoma has already left the closed world and defeated Fever Spirit.

The giants were released to their homes in a manner symbolic of the fact that the human psyche will "re-close." Each individual must, through his or her own heroic effort, repeat the process of emergence from the closed psyche. One person's birth into freedom does not bring about a permanent collapse of the closed system. Each person, in pushing his or her way out of the closed system, achieves his or her own defined and strengthened consciousness. The birth of Makoma's strengthened consciousness enables him to defeat the Fever Spirit. This victory simply confirms that the closed world, for Makoma, has collapsed and that he now exists outside of it. The Fever Spirit, who controlled life and death, symbolized the creator of this closed energy system. The Creator God, or Father God, is often symbolized by the Sun at the zenith of its cycle. Fever Spirit only emerged at midday—when the Sun was at its zenith—and was, therefore, the Creator God. Fever Spirit can be considered the central pillar of this closed system, one that Makoma needed to breach.

Recall that in some of those creation myths presented in chapter I, the organizing God focused upon keeping humans enclosed and ignorant. Such containment conflicts with both the intent of the human-Divine center and the goal of the ally, because both seek their ultimate potential, which lies beyond the enclosure. So when Makoma overthrows the Fever Spirit, he dethrones the Creator God and breaches the closed world. He obtains an opportunity to know the truth of himself. He is encouraged by the spirits of his ancestors, who tell him in a dream to go search for Sakatirini.

Without the prompting by the ancestors, Makoma would have been quite comfortable setting up a home and resting. People's dreams similarly intend to pull them out of ignorance and into action. These ancestor spirits, or voice of the ally, know what Makoma is capable of becoming. So, acting as midwife, they prompt and pull Makoma toward yet another birth, a birth that will occur when Makoma joins with the five-headed Sakatirini, who represents the God-Divine center. This will be the birth of the Divine-Divine center. Makoma has yet to discover his true nature in the mirror of the God-Divine center. We, too, are generally ignorant of our full potential. But through dreams, similar to the voice of ancestor spirits, we are pushed to realize our capabilities.

Makoma's dream directs him to search for five-headed Sakatirini. These five heads are a synthesis of the four giants plus the Fever Spirit. One of the symbolic associations for the number five is the center. But, if we count Sakatirini's heads, arms and legs, we come up with the number nine, a number associated with the Heavens and, therefore, associated with Spirare from the Juglan myth. So, through this combined symbolism of five and nine, we can draw an association between Sakatirini and the God-Divine center. The number nine also symbolizes both end and beginning with a move to a new plane of existence.[15] The understanding of this symbolism foretells the climax of the Makoma story: once joined, Makoma and Sakatirini move beyond the Earth and clouds to a new dimension.

The plight of the God-Divine center in the Makoma story is described as one of being stuck. This is in keeping with the Juglan myth where Spirare is closed, as is Saiwala. Somehow, Sakatirini needs to be extricated from his closed world and he finally receives help from an empowered Makoma. It took tremendous effort to awaken Sakatirini because his attention was drawn toward his own plight; he is unconscious, or what we would call the latent God-Divine. The God's "stuckness" actually relates to his own state of unconsciousness. The Jumping Mouse story gave us this same message: Jumping Mouse, who found Wolf in an unconscious state, brought him into consciousness. In like manner, Makoma awakens Sakatirini with his hammer. Once again, his human-Divine center has played a prominent role in making manifest the God-Divine center. In an Acoma creation story, the first people were instructed to face east. This caused the Sun to rise.[16] In a Hawaiian myth, the coming of people brought day. Both stories confirm the notion that humans are directly related to consciousness, a consciousness with which they can then awaken the God(s).

As soon as Makoma gets Sakatirini's attention, both entities have to overcome the state of growing weary of themselves. Each suffers from isolation. In the Juglan myth, each walnut half becomes lost from the other so that each feels unfinished and alienated. Thus, Sakatirini and Makoma both share a similar psychological danger where growth could cease. The danger existed when Makoma decided to set up a home and rest. And it existed when Sakatirini became unmovable. Likewise, when we decide that we have come far enough, we grow dull and begin to spiritually and psychologically die.

However, if a person responds to the call of his or her spirits, as Mouse and Makoma do, then he or she will be provided the opportunity to come into relationship with the God-Divine. From this relationship, the Divine-Divine center is formed. By demanding Sakatirini's attention, Makoma awakens him and brings him to consciousness. The conscious Sakatirini is then able to enlighten Makoma. Makoma receives a physique equal to Sakatirini as though Sakatirini had cracked Makoma open. Makoma could then see his own true nature. Their equality further unfolds in the matched wrestling as Makoma (the human-Divine center) and Sakatirini (the God-Divine center) interlock and are unable to break away from each other.

Needless to say, it is quite a wrestling match to get a person to look at the possibility of equality with God. Our egos automatically reject the idea of equality, a rejection based on the psyche's collective bias that God is greater than we. If a person can manage to get as far as Makoma has in the journey beyond Jung's first step of individuation, then the Divine-Divine center will be born. The image of this birth lies in the entwined Sakatirini and Makoma as they are taken by the Great Spirit into the realm beyond the world and clouds.

The Great Spirit is the ally and it resides in the psychoid. The combined efforts of Makoma and Sakatirini have brought them into the psychoid home of the Great Spirit, where neither man nor God is any longer bound to their respective closed systems. Makoma and Sakatirini entwined represent the reassembled Juglan or the whole walnut because both halves have rejoined.

Remember, though, that in the Juglan myth a third entity was born, one that must be included in the reunion in order for the manifestation of a Psychoid Self. This third entity is the Great Spirit or ally, whose inclusion into the "whole walnut" is the focus of the following story. "Broken Eggs" came to me in meditation.

Broken Eggs

In a very far-away land lives a very distraught Hen with a very disturbing problem. For, you see, the shaking of the land constantly breaks her eggs. Quite beside herself, she struts about in such a stew that she nearly steps on Worm, who comes above ground to see what all the fuss is about. Seeing Hen's near-fatal step, Worm screams a warning: "Watch out! What is the matter with you this day?"

Hen stops mid-stride and gently sets her foot down, being careful to avoid Worm. Fretfully, Hen explains to Worm about her broken eggs and her complete preoccupation with solving the problem. "I've been so taken by my eggs that I haven't been aware of anything else."

"Ah, misfortune has brought us together, today. I can help with the answer to your broken eggs," exclaims Worm. "Deep within the earth, my homeland, lies the secret to your troubles. It is I that can show you the Way!"

"You are a most unlikely being to come to my aid. Never would I have thought to look to you, Worm. Even if your homeland holds the clue, I could hardly go. I will not fit through your frighteningly dark passageway and my feathers would be forever caked by the dirt and mud." In this way, Hen attempts to deflect Worm's aid.

Worm patiently convinces Hen that the only way to avoid the continuation of her broken eggs is to join together in the search. Hen eventually relents and they begin the journey inward, with Worm burrowing and loosening the ground as Hen scoops away the dirt. In this fashion, Worm and Hen move into the occasionally shaking earth.

After a bit, Hen suddenly realizes that the passageway, which ought to be dark, in fact reflects light. In bringing this to Worm's attention, they both timidly turn about, searching for the light's source. Star's presence shocks them. Worm stammers, "What are you doing here? This is a most unlikely place to find you!"

Star explains about being shaken awake when the two of them joined for this most formidable quest. Pulled strongly by their need, Star fell upon their path, flooding it with light. "Worm, you may know the direction to seek, but I know the one that you must seek, the Great Talker, Maker of All. My light will keep you true to the way. It requires we three to resolve the broken eggs!"

After much toil and time, the three are halted along their path by a vast face that stretches as far as can be seen. It shouts, "Do not look upon me!" And the earth shakes.

Star announces, "Meet the Great Talker."

Worm, who has burrowed a hole into the earth, extricates himself, keeping his back turned and encourages Hen, who has been shaken off her feet by the shout, to pick herself up without looking at the Great Talker. They both scream, "You shake the land and break the eggs with that voice of yours!"

Hen, exasperated, trembling and still not looking, cries, "We have come for your help, Great Talker, Maker of All."

Great Talker then tells them the story of a time, not so long ago, when Star's light filtered through a deep crevice, illuminating Great Talker. Great Talker saw, in that moment, that it had no body. This truth brought on the lamentations that now rock the land and cause Hen's eggs to break. Most importantly, because of the shaking land, Worm and Hen have come to the Great Talker. "You must find me a body! Now turn and see me."

By Star's light, the two turn to see the Great Talker, Maker of All, without a body. So a dire situation now exists for all of them. Worm and Hen know that to keep the eggs from continually breaking, they will surely need to comply with the Great Talker. Hen, Worm, and Great Talker ponder upon their problems when a bit of magic begins to occur. A ring from Worm, a feather from Hen, a word from Great Talker and the sparkle from Star are pulled into a great heart-shaped weaving. It covers them all. As one, the four share this woven heart-body. The beat of this new Heart-Being vibrates into "all that is and is to come." The lamentations cease and the eggs now hatch.

~

This story centers around broken eggs, much like the Juglan myth centers around a prematurely split walnut. The egg, like the Juglan seed, contains potential life. Some creation myths refer to the egg as containing the entire potential universe; and creation then emerges, in time, from the mature egg. Unfortunately, in "Broken Eggs," and in the Juglan myth, the egg's life potential is not given a chance to fully mature. Therefore, life within the egg does not evolve into what it is capable of being. The problem of this unfinished creation parallels Juglan's premature split and unfinished creation.

Hen realizes the seriousness of this problem and so is representative of the human ego. Support for this analogy can be found in a Nigerian creation myth, wherein the God Obatala set a five-toed hen on the back of a snail in order to spread dirt into the solid earth. The number five can symbolize the human being. Dirt appears in several creation myths to form man or woman, hence dirt is synonymous with humans. It follows that since Hen is directly associated with both dirt and the number five, she is also directly associated with humans. Chapter I explained the human symbolic association to consciousness and the fact that consciousness and ego are synonymous. Therefore, Hen symbolizes the human ego.

Hen, the ego, broods over the puzzle of her broken eggs and wants that mystery solved. In like manner, nagging issues stimulate our egos into action. My ethereal visitor left me brooding over the questions of

"Who are you?" and "Why did you come?" These nagging questions drove me into a search for answers. My attention to the questions, or problem, stimulated dreams and meditations intent on helping solve the mystery. In other words, my unconscious was activated. Worm's ascent from below the ground parallels the activation of my unconscious. Worm symbolizes the Self. One of Jung's amplifications for the Self was "worm" which he described as the first form of the phoenix.[17] C. G. Jung also draws comparison to Christ as a worm in *Mysterium Coniunctionis*, "Who is this king of glory? A worm . . ."[18] When Hen and Worm unite, the ego and Self join together, forming a human-Divine center.

Once Hen (ego) and Worm (Self) form this cooperative relationship, Star, symbolic of the ally, makes itself known to them. In the first chapter, the star was related to the psychoid. Remember that in the Hopi creation story, the star existed beyond the fourth emergence; in *The Egyptian Book of the Dead*, the soul journeys beyond the gods to become a star; and, in the *Magical Papyrus*, the star emerges from beyond the open Sun. These give credence to the interpretation of Star as an element of the psychoid in the same way as is the ally. Star or the ally includes itself in Hen and Worm's relationship. With such participation, the ally becomes part of the human-Divine center.

The timing of the ally's appearance in the individuation process is accurately portrayed in "Broken Eggs." Even though the ally might mark a person early in life, it generally does not become a consciously known participant until that person begins the process of individuation where the ego begins to relate to the Self. The formation of an ego-Self relationship or the human-Divine center is essential in order for the ego to absorb the ally's energy, an energy that is incredibly powerful and foreign, and whose unlimited source comes from outside the "closed" system of the human psyche. Without this formation, the ego can become overwhelmed by the intensity of ally energy and risks becoming either inflated or deflated.

Star brings light to Hen and Worm and thus ensures their success. Similarly, the ally aids our focus by lighting the path of individuation and beyond. By projecting dream content that grabs the dreamer's attention, the ally illuminates meaning for the dreamer. Through a series of these attention-grabbing dreams and subsequent individuation work involving active imagination, the ally pulls the dreamer forward with each new understanding. Steadily the dreamer moves toward a gradually increasing conscious awareness.

In "Broken Eggs," a parallel situation occurs when Hen and Worm travel by Star's light to the Great Talker. As they travel, they become conscious by the series of events that led them into their journey, and aware of their necessary involvement in order to stop the eggs from breaking.

However, unbeknownst to Hen, Star's involvement began well before Hen was conscious of its presence. By the end of the story, it is clear that Star's light had actually started things rolling by shedding light on the Great Talker. His reaction to "seeing himself" caused the shaking which brought Hen into action. When people reflect back upon their work or journey of individuation, they often discover a string of connections within their own personal scenarios that begins with the ally.

Recall from the Juglan myth that the truth contained in Memory (ally) leaks into God's psyche as well as the human psyche. Star's light shows the Great Talker that his body was unfinished. God must be brought into consciousness through the assistance of the ally in the same way that man is brought into consciousness. With this acquired consciousness, the ally can bring humans and God face-to-face.

In "Broken Eggs," Star takes Hen and Worm into a direct encounter with the Great Talker, Maker of All. In other words, the human-Divine center comes face-to-face with the God-Divine center, and they become conscious of one another. Similarly in the Juglan myth, the respective centers, which evolve from the two equal halves of the walnut, become conscious of each other prior to their union. In Makoma's story, Sakatirini and Makoma wrestled to become conscious of one another, then left this world united. The ally, like Star, orchestrates this encounter between human and God and their truthful "seeing" of each other. Once they see each other and accept their mutual need of each other, transformation into a Divine-Divine center can occur.

"Broken Eggs" describes this transformation as a magical transfiguration of Hen, Worm, Great Talker, and Star into the Heart-Being. The Heart-Being, with its sparkle from Star, represents EO, the Luminous Tree. Recall in the Juglan myth that the final step of individuation requires the inclusion of the ally in the union of the human-Divine and God-Divine centers. The sparkle from Star symbolizes this inclusion. Star's light that has been the constant catalyst throughout this story leads to the quantum leap of transfiguration into Heart-Being. This quantum leap is within keeping with the original Juglan myth in which the reunited walnut knows itself only briefly to be "Juglan Illuminated" before becoming EO, the Luminous Tree.

The three stories thus presented help to amplify the successive stages of individuation described in the Juglan myth. The first stage of development, as portrayed by the Jumping Mouse story, is one of consciousness first emerging from within the boundaries of a closed human world. The second stage follows with the formation of a relationship and union with God's emerged consciousness. The entwined Makoma and Sakatirini portrayed this stage of development. The now-united consciousness of human and God become a restored wholeness, like the restored walnut in Juglan. However, the process of evolution that the ally is all about demands that we not just return to the original wholeness of the walnut, but that something "other" than this original wholeness must occur. Otherwise, real growth is only an illusion. The ally is that element which entirely changes the restored original wholeness when it unites with the restored wholeness in the final stage of individuation. Since the ally is not part of either half of the original closed system, it changes "originalness," breaks the circular pattern, and frees creation from its closed script.

A person, driven by the desire to truly know who he or she is, and accompanied directly or indirectly by his or her ally, has the opportunity to take the path of divine transformations beyond the first step of individuation into the realm of the psychoid. Once driven onto this path, he or she will be guided by the ally, and will need fortitude, honesty, and trust for the journey.

PART TWO

A Portrait of the Ally

Chapter 4

ANGELS AND THE ALLY

THE PREVIOUS SECTION LAID out the basic model of the new paradigm, from the ego's encounter with the Self to the formation of EO, the Luminous Tree. The mythological motifs found in the fairy tales and myths from around the world revealed that the major elements of the new paradigm existed within the unconscious long before they began to manifest more clearly in our time. The analysis of these stories clarified the nature of the path and the goal sought. The key ingredient, without which this journey toward EO could not be made, is the ally.

In many ways the ally is the most fascinating part of the model presented in the last section. It is the ally as memory that guides the human Self to its manifestation, awakens the Self of God to its dysfunctional state, and binds these two halves together. Moreover, it is with the addition of the ally to the union of human-Divine and God-Divine that the final awesome state is reached, when a new being, a new God emerges as EO.

In order to fully understand the voyage to the Luminous Tree one must understand the ally and its nature. This is doubly important because not only does the ally create the final sought-after condition, it is also the guide and companion on the way from beginning to end. One can work with an ally before the Self manifests, and still be working with that ally when the tree opens to a new world.

In this section, therefore, I will present the nature of the ally and many of its attributes. I shall do so first by contrasting the ally with the popular image of the angel. There are many similarities between the ally and the angel, but there are very significant differences as well. Looking at these similarities and differences will enable us to highlight the basic features that the ally possesses. Furthermore, it is our contention that the emergence of the ally is a momentous event, marking the next stage in the process of spiritual evolution. Casting our eyes back on the previous and related images reveals much of the newness of the ally as it appears today.

Having said that, it is also important to acknowledge that the ally did manifest to individuals in earlier times and their descriptions of these manifestations are useful in rounding out our understanding of the ally. Some of the material about the angels, placed in the right context, reveals some truths about the ally, just as the fairy tales and myths from much earlier times did. Though the ways of understanding these manifestations have evolved, looking to the past can always teach us something about the present. Though I will by necessity be critical of much of the work on angels, as I am attempting to delineate the ally from them, I also respect the work done by those who came before us and who earnestly sought the experience of the psychoid. Therefore, in this chapter, I will focus on several descriptions of encounters with angels with a critical eye, but also with the intent of learning more about the ally.

In the next chapter I shall turn to another, more systematic and long-lasting, attempt to formulate a theory of the psychoid and of the ally. I have studied alchemy for many years and written on it in a previous work, and I have come to respect it as a symbolic expression of the experience of individuation and of the movement into the psychoid. In fact, by studying alchemy, one can discover images for the whole new paradigm.

It may surprise today's reader that anyone would bother with alchemy, as it is a very strange mixture of bizarre images and chemical formulas. The chemical doctrines of alchemy have proven erroneous, but, as Jung has so clearly demonstrated, the symbols of alchemy lay bare the deepest secrets of the human soul.

The overarching quest of the alchemists was to create a magical substance they called the Philosopher's Stone. Once created, the Stone could transmute other metals into gold, heal all physical diseases, and bestow spiritual wisdom. Many alchemists believed that the Stone was actually a material substance created through material processes, but most knew that they were engaged in a spiritual quest. Even those who believed in the efficacy of laboratory work knew that their endeavors had an all-important spiritual dimension. Although the formulations of this spiritual dimension might vary from alchemist to alchemist, alchemy in its purest form was about the transmutation of the soul and of the Divinity. It was especially concerned with the processes of incarnation by which the Divinity found its way into the human psyche.[1] These processes transformed both the Divinity itself and the human psyche in which it established residence. The symbols of alchemy reveal the ways in which the unconscious describes these experiences.

Even though the alchemists themselves did not always understand the full import of the symbols they were using, their writings contain a gold mine of spiritual insights and information that the contemporary student, availing him- or herself of new perspectives about the nature of imagery and psychic reality, will find most useful.

There are several good reasons to suppose that the ally experience and the interaction with the Divine that it represents are unique to the Western psyche, such as its emphasis on individuality, individuation, and evolution. The American and Western European spiritual traditions have been suffering from lack of direction and loss of soul for many years, perhaps because we have nearly forgotten the rich images and practices of our Western mystery traditions. In recent years, this tradition has received renewed interest and been given its own distinct classification as "esoteric religion."

The elements of the esoteric religious tradition, including alchemy, astrology, and the works of such individuals as Jacob Boehme and Rudolph Steiner, have several features in common. As pointed out by Antoine Faivre, these include imagination, the experience of transmutation, and emphasis on nature as a living being.[2]

This trend in religious thought extends back from contemporary times through the Middle Ages to the Classical world, but it has never been the dominant religion. In fact it has often struggled for survival against the repression of collective creeds and state institutions. Nevertheless, in its diverse and profound expressions it gives voice to the unconscious and contains the seeds of a truly Western spiritual path.

One main ingredient of the ancient esoteric tradition is its emphasis on inner experience; according to some of its proponents, every human being contains the source of truth within his or her self. Therefore, the cognitive study of spiritual experience may sometimes seem irrelevant. If all truth comes from within oneself, the study of earlier writers and their theories might seem pointless. It may also seem off-the-mark to spend time thinking about one's experiences; yet profound considerations form an essential ingredient in any deep spiritual exploration.

In terms of ally work and exploring the ally relationship, it is important to realize that we stand in an old and well-respected spiritual tradition. All too frequently, those of us who explore the inner realm can end up feeling alone and isolated and, more often than not, out of synch with the world around us. Anyone who goes against collective wisdom and values confronts feelings of alienation. Such feelings cannot be avoided, but they can be mitigated by the realization that we are in fact not alone; that others have had similar experiences and written about them over the centuries. I have read several alchemists' dreams in which they experience an inner ally figure who reveals information and provides insight. The same type of dream experience can happen to a person today, when his or her ally comes to teach the person about his or her life or path. To know that these experiences have been occurring to others for hundreds of years is very reassuring.

There is an additional reason to refer to older material when talking about the ally. If one is careless, one can be fooled by one's inner experience. Working with one's own experiences can convey a feeling of absolute certainty, but a look at the history of the esoteric spiritual tradition reveals many examples of people who lost themselves to inflation and delusion. Men like Giordano Bruno became so enamored of their own ideas and so convinced of their central importance for the spiritual well being of the world that they became lost in their delusions of being the next savior or founder of the new religion for which the world eagerly waited. It appears that Bruno even hoped to convert the Pope and all Catholicism to his way of thinking. Bruno paid for his delusion with his life. Inflation does not always take one's life, but it always has a deleterious affect.

I was very fortunate to have a partner who was exploring her own similar experiences. We were able to balance each other many times. Moreover, the opportunity to work with hundreds of clients has taught me more than I can say, and I am indebted to each of them for what they contributed to my understanding of the psyche and of the ally.

For all of these reasons it is wise to consult the writings of the past and I shall study the writings of those of the esoteric tradition in this chapter in regards to their views on angels and in the next chapter as to how the alchemists perceived an ally figure. In both cases we shall learn a great deal about the nature of the ally and about what makes it unique.

Is the Ally an Angel?

Whenever I lecture on the ally, someone in my audience usually asks me the question, "How does the ally relate to angels?" In the last few years, angels have become a topic of great interest to the general public, with New Age books, movies, and TV shows increasing their popularity. I believe angels are more popular now for two main reasons. In our world of uncertainty and spiritual confusion, people often seek a reassuring image that offers them a sense of protection and security. Angels— above all other spiritual images—provide the reassurance we seek, for they are spiritual beings concerned with humanity's welfare. Angels are also popular because we have a great hunger for spiritual experience and contact with beings of the spiritual world.

The popularization of angels has a downside, however. Much of the current literature so popularizes angels that it tames them, and makes them seem like a caricature of real psychoidal entities. In addition, it creates confusion when the idea of the ally crops up, for the ally is different in significant respects from angels. Yet, part of the purpose of this book is to present the reality of the ally as well as other psychoidal beings. Earlier traditions had definite ideas about angels as spiritual entities and can shed light on the nature of the ally through both contrast and comparison.

The literature on angels is vast and much of it fascinating. Studying it has clarified my own ideas about the nature of the ally and of the psychoid. Unfortunately, I cannot discuss all of the traditions I have studied, so I will confine myself to those that are among the most significant. I shall present the ideas and experiences of John Dee, Rudolf Steiner, New Age writings, and finally, the Sufi mystics.

JOHN DEE (1527-CA. 1609)

John Dee is one of the more interesting figures of the 16th century. He was an alchemist, a natural philosopher, a mathematician, an astrologer, an advisor to Elizabeth I of England, and a dedicated communicator with angels. However, unlike the other writers I shall consider in this chapter, John Dee did not know how to communicate with angels directly. As was customary in his day, he used other people to speak with angels for him. These individuals, known as scryers, would gaze into water or crystals and experience angels both visually and verbally. Dee would ask the angels questions through his scryers, who would respond with the words of the angels. This would be akin to my asking someone to do an active imagination for me in order to answer my own questions. It also resembles the current practice of channeling, in which individuals ask the channeler to give them answers derived from higher sources. It should be pointed out that it is impossible to create a relationship with a psychoidal being, and especially an ally, through a surrogate. However, Dee was not really interested in creating a relationship with the angels, but in gaining wisdom from them, and in helping them bring about an apocalyptic revolution in the world. Dee's experiences with the angels indicate the dangers, as well as some of the advantages, of working with spiritual forces and they also show clearly the difference between angels as he saw them and the ally.

Dee's quest was wisdom. He, like his contemporaries, considered nature a book that, if read correctly, revealed the secrets of the Divinity and the ways in which the Divine manifested in the world. After years of study, he came to believe that the best way to acquire this knowledge was to gain it from angels.

For Dee, angels were intermediate beings existing "between God and humans, celestial and terrestrial, sacred and mundane."[3] It is interesting that Dee places angels in this intermediate state, which we have recognized as belonging to the psychoid. He felt that God communicated through the angels to certain individuals about certain significant events. But Dee did not want limited encounters with angels; he sought on-going dialogues. In short, he wanted to do active imagination with the angels, on a regular basis, with the help of his scryers. Deborah Harkness refers to his interaction with the angels as "conversations,"[4] which have a parallel to active imagination in which the ego talks with an inner figure.

Dee's conversations were quite intricate and detailed. The angels instructed him on the creation of certain signs and magical objects that he needed in order to work with them. He sought their knowledge about alchemy and the preparation of the Philosopher's Stone. In this, he was much like other alchemists, as we shall see in the next chapter, for the alchemists believed that only Divine revelation would secure success in their work. The conversation with the angels about alchemy is very interesting, though ultimately frustrating for both Dee and the reader, for the angels reveal little of substance. Nevertheless, the quest for knowledge that initially marked Dee's endeavors is a legitimate reason for contacting spiritual beings. Unfortunately, Dee's angels also conveyed spurious information, such as instructing Dee to share wives with his scryer Edward Kelly. Dee apparently followed the directions of the angels in everything, though he also could challenge them on occasion. His conversations reveal two major weaknesses that apply to anyone attempting active imagination. When one receives information that violates one's personal feeling, it is a mistake to accept or act on it. If, for example, Dee felt it wrong to swap wives, he should have refused no matter what, otherwise too much power would have been afforded the beings with whom he was dialoguing. Furthermore, the quest for knowledge soon drifted in the direction of preparing for the coming apocalypse and a definite sign of inflation crept into Dee's conversations. The angels let him know that he was instrumental in preparing the world for the next age and it was his work to convince the rulers of Europe that they should follow the teachings of the angels or face dire consequences. His conversations moved from the personal quest for knowledge to the salvation of the world, with Dee as the one doing the saving. This type of inflation is all too common in work with the psychoid, and even enters, at times, into the work with the ally. Being in touch with powerful beings tempts the human participant to identify with that power, even if only by becoming their spokesperson for the world. Dee fell for this, and it landed him in trouble with both church and state.

Dee also fell into the trap of using active imagination with his angels to predict future events, and the future of individuals he knew personally. These predictions were only occasionally correct, but using psychoidal powers to predict the future normally activates the trickster in them, and they lie as often as they tell the truth. I remember getting hooked while I was in Zurich by the desire to know what would happen to my father, and the inner figure with whom I was talking assured me most earnestly my father would be dead within a year. This was a complete falsehood, though it had some relevance to my *inner* father. The more one tries to use either psychoidal or inner figures for power purposes, the more problems arise.

Though these dialogues tricked Dee, there is no reason to doubt that they were real active imagination experiences. Dee, himself, was certainly sincere, and though historians have grave doubts about the sincerity of Edward Kelly, my understanding of these dialogues is that they were genuine active imagination experiences. Especially in his earlier work, Dee's conviction that angels possessed supernatural wisdom about the workings of the world motivated him to seek their help. Angels were the messengers of God who could deliver information about the workings of the world, but also revelations of God's word and truth. Thus, angels were quite capable of revealing Divine secrets. They were guides, as well, who would advise Dee on the right course of action and reprimand him when he went astray. In their role as conveyers of wisdom and revealers of Divine secrets, they are like the ally, who often plays these roles as well. For this reason, Dee's interaction with the angels is informative and applicable to working with an ally.

Unfortunately, as mentioned, we can learn mostly what *not* to do from Dee. We must beware of inflation and we must neither identify nor use the power of the ally for our own designs, even if those designs include helping the world at large. What we discuss with the ally most often concerns ourselves and our work, and when such discussion relates to issues beyond our personal ones, it is for our information only, not for us to spread abroad as universal truth. The ally and our union with it are incredibly personal and intimate. One finds no such union or intimacy in Dee's work with the angels.

The angels that he encountered were archetypal forces such as Gabriel, or Uriel, and Dee never seemed to consider having a personal relationship with them. This is typical of work with archetypes or with spirits that are not allies. They never bring up the possibility of relationship. Dee's angels were impersonal forces, possessed of wisdom and some power, but not adverse to trickery and outright lying. Moreover, like impersonal forces, they were given to grandiloquent statements that are biblical in sound and character:

Behold sayeth your God, I am a Circle on Whose hands stand 12 Kingdomes: Six are seats of living breath: the rest are as sharp sickles: or the horns of death wherein the Creatures of

ye earth are to are not [*sic*] Except myne own hand which slipe
and shall ryse. In the first I made you Stuards and placed you
in seats 12 of government giving unto every one of you power
successively over 456 the true ages of tyme [5]

What in the world does all that mean? Much of Dee's conversations are
of this nature and scholars still debate their meaning. To be sure, a symbolic study of such words would probably reveal something meaningful, but active imagination should be direct and to the point, and not
leave one feeling bewildered. The angels seem to be indicating their
ability to reveal truths as profound and reliable as those found in biblical revelations. But, once more, these are of an impersonal nature, and
are more confusing than helpful, and so do not resemble encounters
with allies at all.

As Harkness demonstrates, Dee's angels were "important, divine
members of the cosmic structure. The best-known angels in Dee's conversations are the archangels of the Judeo-Christian tradition: Gabriel,
Michael, Raphael, and Uriel."[6] As parts of the cosmic structure, these
angels most resemble archetypes or their psychoidal correlates. They have
no real personal identity and are simply messengers. There is no possibility of developing a relationship with them, and no suggestion of union
or transformation. They are good examples of psychoidal entities that
appear to convey specific information and reveal certain powers. They are,
however, neither free beings able to change their roles nor individuate in
any fashion, and in these aspects they differ greatly from the ally.

About the only thing these angels have in common with the ally is
that one can dialogue with them in order to gain wisdom and to seek

advice. Since, however, there is no personal relationship with them, one must always be careful about taking the advice they give. One should never take such information at face value, or follow it naively. Rather, one should test the messages repeatedly to see if they are genuine and wait for results. If what such impersonal figures teach proves to be untrue, they will make up many excuses for why this is so. Usually, they claim the person they talked to failed to act or understand correctly. It is wrong to believe such explanations, and should they give erroneous information again, it is wise to discontinue any contact with them. If they communicate in such abstract language that one cannot understand what they are saying, it is also best to treat them with suspicion.

The other trick that such impersonal beings play is to create inflation, and to cause one to loose sight of one's own limitations or personal characteristics. They like to inform individuals, as they did Dee, that the individuals are very special and have an important role to play in world events. The best way to handle such information is with humor—laugh at them and yourself for believing you could be so important or powerful. Spiritual work is rarely about power, so if conversations often portray one's great importance or influence, something is off. I do not believe impersonal figures trick with malice, but being impersonal, they take no account of the personality of the human being and tend to obscure normal, ordinary issues in favor of large, impersonal ones. Even if all that they told Dee had been true, he was foolish to listen. Even if we could play a major role in history, so could many others. During Dee's time, he was not the only person to be told that he was instrumental in the coming apocalypse. Many thought of themselves as indispensable in the role they had to play. They would be no more right or wrong than Dee, for all were receiving messages of an impersonal character that had little to do with them as human beings. Working with impersonal forces can be interesting, but is often very dangerous. Dee's motives in seeking wisdom and in bringing spiritual forces to bear on worldly problems were justified, but he soon ran afoul of the impersonal nature of the beings with whom he conversed.

The collective unconscious and the related impersonal forces of the psychoid reveal truths that are of a universal sort. They reveal truths that belong to the age in which one lives. Dee, for example, learned that he needed to work for religious harmony. His age was one of religious intolerance and persecution that would culminate in dreadful wars. The angels were right that he needed to work for religious tolerance, and many individuals of his epoch, such as Giordano Bruno, were given the same task. It could be said that every individual of that time needed to work for religious freedom and tolerance. Unfortunately, Dee, like so many others, thought that this made him special and that he should convince monarchs to listen to the angels, with predictable results. Bruno, too, thought he had a mission to convert the world to his way of thinking, and was burned at the stake for his troubles. When dealing with issues of our time, we should take them seriously, but we must find a way to personalize them, rather than identify with them at the expense of our personality. Dee was not the bringer of religious harmony he imagined, but he might have personalized his messages by living in harmony with others, honoring people of all faiths, and perhaps even writing on the need for religious harmony. He could have done all these things as one wise man, not as a prophet speaking for angelic powers, nor as the transmitter of Divine revelation.

RUDOLF STEINER (1861-1925)

Rudolf Steiner was a prolific writer who had a tremendous impact on the world of esoteric studies and on children's education. He presented a very complicated system in many books and there is no room to cover it all here. I have extracted his ideas about angels to their outlines, which will still give us further insight into the nature of psychoidal beings and the way in which angels differ from allies.

Steiner's ideas about angels are similar to Dee's in that he saw in them impersonal forces. Unlike Dee, however, he seemed to think that angels were difficult to encounter. In order to access the angel's realm consciously, one must undergo transformation and attain a higher state of consciousness. Conversations with angels occur all the time, but, for the vast majority of people, only during sleep. Angelic forces cannot reach people in waking states, but when consciousness detaches from the sleeping body, it encounters these forces.

Though it is difficult to directly experience angels while awake, it is essential for individuals to work with them. An evolutionary process has made contact between individuals and angels important, because the heavenly hierarchies no longer communicate with the human race as a whole but only with individuals. In the introduction to a collection of Steiner's lectures on angels, Wolf-Ulrich Klunker argued that "we can no longer talk of a relationship between humanity and higher beings, but only of one formed between them and an individual person. The reality of the hierarchies is now, and will be in the future, founded on spiritual individuality."[7] In other words, while the angelic hierarchies remain the same, they no longer relate to humanity as a whole, but to individual people. This introduces an element of the personal missing from Dee's communication, and also tends to mitigate against inflation, since any individual can relate to the angels if he or she first learns to think of himself or herself as a differentiated individual who did not simply belong to humanity as a mass. The individuating person must learn to relate to the angels as an individual who is aware of his or her own spiritual processes and transformations. This represents a significant movement past Dee's mode of relating to the angels.

On the other hand, Steiner did not believe that the angels were material in any sense, but spiritual beings that one could not directly perceive. They do not belong to the psychoid, since they have nothing material about them, and they make their influences felt only indirectly since they do not come into contact with the physical world. However, I believe that Steiner meant that the angels form images that one can perceive, at least with a sufficiently developed ego consciousness. In Steiner's terminology of the occult, the angels shape images in "the human astral body under the guidance of the Spirits of Form."[8] Apparently, the Spirits of Form have a plan for mankind that they strive to achieve through the agency of the angels. The angels plant images in the astral body. In time, through evolution, these images will manifest in the world. It takes a "thinking developed to become clairvoyant"[9] to perceive these images in the astral body.

The angels plant images designed to further three objectives: to create a brotherhood of humanity; to create visionary insight in every human being so that they may see the divinity in all others; and to develop thinking so deeply that one perceives spiritual beings directly. The angels perform all of their work in the astral body in order to achieve these goals.

There are other spiritual beings that resist the work of the angels. One type tries to help human beings reach spiritual depth, but only at the cost of their individuality, while the other type tries to destroy human spiritual evolution completely. For Steiner, spiritual evolution that does not take place within the individual is of no great value. In this he clearly resembles Jung, and, in his honoring of the individual, recognizes something of the divinity of the Self.

Some of his ideas resemble those presented in this book. The astral body would correspond to the imagination, in which the psychoidal beings manifest through creating images. By doing so they promote the evolution of the human race, but especially of the individual who must develop thinking, or consciousness, of such depth that he or she can perceive the spiritual forces directly. In terms of the individuation process and the relationship of the individual with the spiritual world, there is much in Steiner's teaching that helps us understand the new paradigm. However, despite his emphasis on the individual human being's evolution, there is still no conception of transformation on the part of the angels, nor any sense of an abiding union between human and angel.

Interestingly, Steiner does introduce the concept of the genius, which forms the main image in the next chapter. He even refers to Paracelsus, so he seems to have been familiar with the alchemical idea of the genius that I believe is one model for the ally. I will discuss many aspects of the genius as the alchemists experienced it, for by understanding the genius, we understand the ally. Steiner equates the genius with the Spirit Self that may be carried by a particular angel who will help the human being develop into his Spirit Self. He says of the alchemists that the genius they saw was "nothing but the evolving Spirit

Self, though it is borne by a spirit from the hierarchy of the Angels."[10]

For Steiner, the angel was a self-figure, into which a human would grow at a certain period of evolution. This relates a particular human being with a particular angel, but it is unclear what happens to the angel when the human being reaches this stage of development. Presumably it will no longer carry the Spirit Self and would not be needed any longer. Furthermore, the Spirit Self is not the highest level of development for a human being who goes on to become Life Spirit and Spirit Man. The genius is "nothing but" a stage in the evolutionary process and not the highest one at that.

On the other hand, alchemists saw in the genius a spirit of great power and wisdom with whom they could form a personal relationship. The genius in alchemy was not a "nothing but"; instead it was a spiritual being of the highest value. Steiner's view of the genius diverges from the one we present later, and is different from the ally for several reasons. First of all, the ally is not the self, but other than the self, though related to it as one twin to another. Secondly, the ally does not embody the human Self, but mirrors it only. Thirdly, the ally transforms as the human being does, and they evolve together forever. Finally, the ally enters into union with its human partner. Steiner's conception of the angel more resembles the messenger of Dee than it does the ally, for the angel delivers images to the astral body in order to guide evolution. It carries the guiding messages of the Spirits of Form. There is no apparent transformation of the angels nor is there union between them and the human being. These angels are, once more, impersonal forces, so that Steiner could even speak of the spirits of Nations, archangels that govern the destiny of countries.

However, this is not the end of the story, for Steiner did believe that each of us has his or her own angel, and that we can form a relationship to this angel. To understand this, we must recall that only highly developed thinking perceives the spirit world directly. Very few of us possess this developed thinking, so most relate to the world of the angels during sleep. The angels place the images that guide the human evolutionary process in our astral body, and we experience these images while we are sleeping. However, if we form the correct relationship with our particular angel and to the higher spiritual beings, our astral body can rise in sleep to the realm of the spirits and "enter into a relationship with the world of the spirit that allows [us] to live [our] life from death to rebirth in the right way."[11] Each of us forms a relationship with his or her angel by living the right way, living in a loving, open, and generous way. The angel examines our thoughts and feelings, apparently to evaluate them. After death, the angel passes this information on to the higher authorities that deal with us accordingly.

It is hard for me to say, from what I have read in Steiner's work, just what the relationship to the angel consists of. However, I have found no mention of love, union or transformation of the angel, which are all characteristics of the ally. Moreover, the relationship is governed by correct thinking and there is clearly a perfectionist streak that enters at this point. To evolve, we must be loving, kind, and compassionate, and our thoughts are judged in the afterlife. There is no parallel with the Jungian notion of the shadow in Steiner's vision, never mind the need to honor it. In addition, there is no possibility of relating to the angels in our waking life, in our ordinary and most imperfect lives. The technique of active imagination is not found in Steiner's description of the relationship between human and spirit; we must sleep in order to relate. As Steiner himself admits, this is less than satisfactory, since our consciousness is dimmed in sleep. However, with the evolution of our thoughts, we can rise to the astral level while asleep, apparently with much more self-awareness than is usual in the sleep state.

Steiner's angels are impersonal beings, with a set place, in a set hierarchy, carrying out specific instructions to plant in the human being images that guide spiritual evolution. There exists no possibility for a direct, waking relationship to the angel, and no union with it. The angel does not transform and reveals no individual characteristics. There is thus only little resemblance between the angel and the ally. Despite this, I found Steiner's view of angels much more sophisticated than Dee's. In addition, Steiner's emphasis on the individual human being is noteworthy. Finally, I detected no inflation in Steiner and no sense that he thought that the angels came to him alone, but that he saw himself as a spokesman for all humans seeking spiritual evolution. He did not try to use the angels to effect material change within the world, either for personal gain or for political change. He believed that the world would change as humans followed their angelic instructors and evolved into the higher forms of their being. Though different from the ally and the paradigm presented here, there is much to respect in Steiner's presentation of the angels.

THE NEW AGE

Terry Lynn Taylor is a well-known proponent of the theory of angels as found in the New Age. Her style and content are exemplary of the writings of many New Agers. She does an admirable job of presenting a faulty concept, and the criticisms I offer are not aimed at her directly but at the the concept she espouses. Unfortunately, the New Age thinkers influence most people who are interested in angels, fostering a simplistic and almost Disney-like image of angels and other spiritual beings.

Taylor presents her views in *Messengers of Light*. Essentially, she argues that angels are everywhere, and people who are attuned to them are followed by a flock of angels wherever they go. Angels can appear in any form, even materially, and often as human beings. Her angels are like the TV angels who go around helping people and leading them to the light. In her definition, angels are "heaven-sent agents who are always available to help you create heaven in your life."[12] She expands on this in an interesting passage:

> Let us consider that angels exist in heaven as separate beings of the highest Divine powers in the universe. They are beings of light who send information and loving thoughts through our higher self to inspire and guide us.[13]

These angels are separate beings rather than part of the human being, and in this they resemble the denizens of the psychoid world. They are formed of light, much like the angels of the Sufis, and they send loving thoughts and information to us through the higher self, much like Steiner's angels. This is not a bad definition, with its distinction between higher self and angel and its emphasis on communication through image and intuition. Unfortunately, Taylor descends from this relatively high level to the idea of the angel as a happy-go-lucky being that so loves us that it wants us to be happy all the time, too. In fact, if one thinks happy thoughts, angels are attracted, while they apparently do not like pain and suffering at all. If Steiner ignores the shadow, or the dark side of life, Taylor wipes it out. As with Steiner, angels like loving and compassionate thoughts, and if one develops an optimistic attitude and unconditional love, angels are sure to come. However, we need not sleep to meet the angels; we can meet them in our daily life as physical beings, as well as through our intuitions. Angels are like thoughts and they beam their messages to us. They work for God "to maintain the loving order of the universe."[14] God wants us to be happy and angels help us create happiness on Earth.

There are also guardian angels assigned to protect specific individuals. At moments of crisis, they provide protection and may call in other angels to help as well. So protective and powerful are these angels that we wonder how any bad thing ever happens! How do children die of leukemia, and teenagers murder other teenagers? There seems to be no room for evil thoughts, let alone evil deeds in this world of angels. Of course, if we think evil thoughts and are nasty, the angels may leave, making it likely that they are only effective in helping those who are happy all the time.

In summary, the New Age view of angels is essentially one of heavenly beings of light and love, whose only purpose is to help people be happy and to create heaven on Earth. They are attracted to happy thoughts and loving hearts and repelled by darkness of any kind. They protect us and inspire us with intuitions and guidance.

The ally does inspire with intuition and guidance, and the ally is an independent being separate from the human Self. Often, the ally appears as light, but its goal is not to make us happy. Its goal is transformation and growth, and anyone who transforms knows that suffering is part of the process. Taylor's insistence that "[s]uffering is not a virtue. Suffering means you are subjecting yourself to pain, loss, damage, and disadvantage,"[15] is New Age dogma at its worst, in which light and happiness are the only virtues, while suffering and disease are self-inflicted wounds that one should avoid at all costs. It is not in your control to eliminate suffering. Suffering is part of life and part of the individuation process, and not something that you subject yourself to.

The ally neither creates suffering nor avoids it. It suffers as we do, as we work together to unite and heal the wounds of the Divinity. God is not a perfectly happy Ruler who sends his happy little angels to make us happy. Such a view is as revolting as it is common. If we try to live in the real world, we must come to grips with pain, evil, and darkness; they only get worse if we pretend they don't exist. We must transform them and grow through them. The human Self is not pure light; it is a mixture of light and dark. The light and the dark need not war with each other, but can find harmony and balance if consciousness broadens sufficiently to include both. Nor is the ally a "good" being; it is an entity that seems to unite all the opposites. The ally can be pushy and demanding and sometimes hurt its partner by insisting on growth and development. The ally never "injures," but it can hurt. Nor does our suffering repel it. I have seen repeated instances of allies appearing at times of the greatest pain and suffering. They come neither to heal nor to disperse the pain, but to help us learn from it.

Unfortunately, there is very little to learn about the ally from New Age theories of the angels. If one wishes to make happiness the goal of one's life, one might seek such angels. But, in my years as an analyst, working with hundreds of people, I have learned that those who make happiness the goal are the ones least likely to find it, while those who embrace life full-on, and seek meaning in its vicissitudes, develop a peace and a contentment far superior to happiness as defined by Taylor. To paraphrase Jung, we do not find enlightenment by imagining pictures of light but by bringing light into the darkness.

THE SUFIS AND ANGELS

The Sufi angelic tradition is the most profound I have studied and the most closely related to the ideas of the ally we explore in this book. The tradition of the angels goes back for centuries among the Sufis and likely predates the rise of Islam in Iran. There is a vast literature and many ideas worth considering, but I shall examine only two Sufi traditions: those of Avicenna and of Sohravardi. I use for my source the works of Henry Corbin, who discusses these theories with great depth and insight, and presents samples of the original writings of these two sages.

In his book *Avicenna and the Visionary Recital*, Henry Corbin presents Avicenna's ideas, especially as they relate to angels. Corbin analyzes Avicenna's poetic work *Recital of the Bird*, while explaining the theories that put it in context. Avicenna's vision of the angel so resembles ally theory that they are almost indistinguishable. Discussing the archetypal model of the *Recital of the Bird*, which has much in common with other visionary works of the Sufis, Corbin explains that the soul, seeking spiritual connection, often finds itself alone and alienated from the world. It is at this point that "a *personal* figure appears on its horizon, a figure that announces itself to the soul *personally* because it symbolizes *with* the soul's most intimate depths. In other words, the soul discovers itself to be the earthly counterpart of another being with which it forms a totality that is dual in structure. The two elements of this dualitude may be called the ego and the Self, or the transcendent celestial Self and the earthly Self, or by still other names."[16] The two names used in this book are Self and ally, for, as the angel that the soul meets on its visionary quest forms a totality with it, so, too, the Self and the ally form a totality. Neither is complete without the other. Corbin italicizes the words "personal" and "personally" to indicate the importance of the individuality of the angel. This is not an impersonal, archetypal angel such as those we have met before; this angel is a personality. It is a living being, independent of the psyche of the seeker, and, according to Henry Corbin, is an individual expression of the Holy Spirit and the guardian angel, guide, and even savior of the seeker. The Holy Spirit individuates into a single angelic being, which in turn individuates through its relationship with the seeker. Corbin explains that in a culminating vision there occurs a simultaneous individuation of the soul and of the angelic figure that appears in the vision.[17] There are thus two stages in the individuation process of the guardian angel: it emerges from the Holy Spirit and then transforms in the visionary encounter with its human partner. This imagery corresponds almost totally with the idea that the ally emerges from the Divine world and then undergoes transformation through the relationship with its partner. The guardian angel is not only personal; it transforms as well.

There are other remarkable parallels. In the *Recital*, when the human traveler meets the angel, the latter reveals his name and what he does. As we shall see in chapter 6, one of the first stages in working with an ally is to learn its name, for it marks the beginning of a personal relationship. The angel guides the seeker to the heavenly palace, the goal of the journey, just as the ally guides the Self to union with God. However, there are differences that remain between the Sufi model and the model presented here.

William Chittick warns that Corbin over-emphasized the idea of the individuality of the angels, making it seem that each was a god unto itself, and neglected the essential feature of Islam: its monotheism and its declaration that Allah alone is God. Chittick also criticizes Jungians for giving the soul's imaginative powers too much credit.[18] This suggests that, while the ally goes on to transform the God-Divine, there is in the Sufi tradition no sense of Allah's transformation. Yet there is still no question that, as the incarnation of the Holy Spirit, the angel is intimately related to Allah and does, itself, transform.

Corbin writes in a similar vein in his book, *The Man of Light in Iranian Sufism*. In this work he presents the theories of Shihaboddin Yahya Sohravardi, a Sufi who died in the 12th century and who was one of the teachers of Ibn 'Arabi. Sohravardi taught that the essence of the human being was an inner man of light, but that this man of light has a celestial counterpart, an angelic being of light. This is the "invisible Guide, the heavenly Partner, the 'Holy Spirit' of the itinerant mystic . . . the Figure of light, the Image and the mirror in which the mystic contemplates—and without which he could not contemplate—the theophany (*tajalli*) *in the form corresponding to his being*."[19] The italics are again Corbin's, and once more reflect his emphasis on the individuality of the Sufi gnosis. The angel is the being of light that not only guides but also reveals the Divinity of the mystic and his or her own individual relationship to

God. The angel reveals the nature of God in the form that most corresponds to the being of the mystic. The angel is thus an individualized God whose form is ideally suited to the nature of the mystic. This, too, reflects on the nature of the ally, whose form always relates to the nature and the needs of its human partner. Sohravardi calls the angel the Perfect Nature, which he defines as the "heavenly entity, the philosopher's Angel, conjoined with his star, which rules him and opens the doors of wisdom for him, teaches him what is difficult, reveals to him what is right, in sleeping and in waking."[20]

Everything said of the Perfect Nature is true of the ally. It is the guide and the teacher who reveals right and wrong in sleeping and in waking. Moreover, it is conjoined with its partner's star, which means it is intimately related to its partner's Self. Now, despite Chittick's warning, it seems that Sohravardi saw union with the angel as the highest of spiritual goals. He wrote a prayer directed to his angel:

> Thou, my lord and prince, my most holy angel, my precious spiritual being, Thou are the Spirit who gave birth to me, and Thou art the Child to whom my spirit gives birth . . . Thou who art clothed in the most brilliant of divine Lights . . . may Thou manifest thyself to me in the most beautiful . . . of epiphanies, show me the light of Thy dazzling face, be for me the mediator . . . lift the veils of darkness from my heart.[21]

This is a heartfelt and beautiful expression of love for the angel and the possibility of union. Corbin expressed his belief that a union occurred between the heavenly angel and the mystic, a union he believed was expressed by the formula I x I = I. This formula makes it clear that the two partners in the union retain their individuality while coming together to form one being.[22]

Not being a Sufi scholar I cannot say whether or not Chittick is correct in his criticism of Corbin, but even if we accept the idea that the depiction of union with the angel is Sufism seen through the eyes of Corbin, there is still no doubt that some of the Sufis held the angel in highest regard and attributed to it characteristics that are related to those of the ally. Furthermore, even if this idea were all of Corbin's invention, which I doubt, it offers a remarkable parallel to the ideas formulated in our book.

Unlike the other images of angels we have reviewed, there is a clear sense of union between human and angel and a strong suggestion that the angel, as well as its partner, is transformed through this union. Furthermore, the angel appears as a specific form in the imagination of the mystic. Emerging from the Holy Spirit, or the world of pure spirit, it first takes on form, or in our terminology, enters the psychoid, and then individuates in harmony with the Sufi who has received it. Every aspect of this motif fits the experience of the ally. We have found in the Sufi tradition of the guardian angel the clearest forerunner of the ally. There are others, for Iranian mysticism owes much to the Zoroastrian tradition and its notion of the Divine twin, but we can conclude our review of angelic imagery by noting that even in the Sufi school there are differences from the view of the ally presented here.

In our view, the ally comes to initiate three phases of spiritual work. It supports the process of individuation whereby the individual discovers his or her own inner Divine core. It brings together the God-Divine with the human-Divine. This later work implies the imperfection of God and Its need to unite with the human being to find Its totality. Finally, the ally enters the union of God and human and all are transformed into a third being, EO. I have not found any trace of this last transformation in any of the earlier traditions, though there may be some hints of it in Sufism. But for any Islamic mystic the conception of an imperfect God is dangerous, if not inconceivable. This is not to deny that it is present, for Western practicioners of Sufism have told me that there is such an idea. I myself have not found it in Sufi writings though. It is an element definitely missing from the other traditions we have examined in this chapter.

Traditions that are centuries old have conceptions of spiritual beings and spiritual realities that relate to the ally and the psychoid. But there are none in which the angel completely conforms to our experience of the ally, or in which union with the angel implies the transformation of God. The theory of the ally is unique, and represents a new phase in spiritual evolution of both humanity and divinity. Now, let us turn to examine the nature of the ally.

Chapter 5

THE ALLY IN THE ALCHEMICAL TRADITION

ONE OF THE FASCINATING things about being an analyst and analyzing hundreds of dreams every year is being privy to the workings of the collective unconscious. Listening to dreams every day allows the analyst to witness the wisdom that arises from the inner world of the human soul. Some truths that emanate from the unconscious are unique to a particular individual, while others are timeless and speak to people everywhere. Some present information as old as humanity, while others portray new material that reveals the evolutionary flux of spiritual development. Dreams of the ally belong in the later category, and show a movement within the collective unconscious toward a new spiritual orientation and principle.

Ally dreams include meetings with magical animals and spiritual entities and are characterized by the feelings of love they engender. The dreamer not only feels a deep sense of love, but an invitation to union and companionship unlike anything he or she has previously experienced. For example, one client dreamed of a buffalo that walked into her room and gazed into her eyes, filling her with ecstasy and joy. Another dreamed of a wild cat that stalked the dreamer as she walked through the woods, then leapt on her, only to begin frolicking and wrestling. She awoke with delight. A third dreamed of a numinous being of light who said to him sadly that he had been waiting for him all his life. The dreamer felt a wrenching pain as he realized he had lived so long alone, without the companionship of this light being. Such dreams are often followed by other dreams or active imagination experiences in which the union hinted at originally flowers into an on-going relationship. After working with many individuals with such dreams and waking encounters, I decided to begin teaching about the ally experience.

Though I had worked with my own ally for many years, I hesitated to lecture about such experiences until I had the opportunity to consider other people's ally encounters. I was uncertain if my meetings with the ally were unique to me, or indicated a more general phenomenon. I observed carefully my clients' dreams and listened to their experiences of active imagination. Furthermore, as I began to lecture publicly, I heard stories from a great many people about their own connections with allies. Though they did not use the word "ally," and often did not know how to understand the nature of their experiences, their reports were all remarkably similar. In this fashion, I gained certainty that many others had ally encounters similar to my own. Once I was clear about this, I began to study more about the ally, its symbolism, and the nature of its wisdom. Through our collaboration, Linda Vocatura and I developed a theory that fits the experiences we have observed. However, work with the ally is always evolving and leading to deeper insights. In addition, the ally comes in unique ways to each individual, so general formulations must be made carefully and respectfully. I present them not in a dogmatic spirit, but as tentative ideas about a new and unfolding process.

Rather than presenting a fully elaborated theoretical system about the ally, I offer what the alchemists of the Middle Ages termed *theoria*; ideas based on experiences, which lead, in turn, to new experiences. Correct understanding of one's inner communication sets the stage for further discoveries. Although I refer in this chapter to the wisdom of earlier times, I base all that I write on my own and other contemporary people's experiences. My hope is that the ideas outlined here will lead readers to recognize and understand similar experiences of their own.

The *theoria* that emerged from our efforts concerns the ally, its nature, the relationship that one can create with it and, on a larger scale, the transformation of the ways in which the human and Divine interact. As mentioned, the overall theory owes its major components to direct experience; however, it has been very interesting to study earlier spiritual traditions to see what they might reveal about the ally experience. Though there is no one tradition that covers all of what is presented here as ally theory, there are elements of our theory that can be traced back to earlier ideas. This is especially true of the hermetic tradition in the West and, principally, of the spiritual doctrine known as alchemy.

The inner light of Nature that creates dreams and symbolic expression does not lie, and in Her teachings one can look for a deeper understanding of personal experience. Although the interpretation of such imagery is, of course, the expression of the interpreter, contemplation of the images created by the psyche over the centuries helps to reflect the deeper nature of one's own experiences. Combining personal experience with study is an invaluable aid to the student of inner exploration. I once heard that Jung said that to explore the unconscious successfully one needed, above all else, a sense of humor and great patience. To those invaluable assets I would add an ability to remain objective about one's discoveries. It is not at all easy, but retaining an objective ability to challenge, criticize, and review one's own understandings is essential in inner work. An objective, critical view of the nature of one's experience, and an objective study of symbolic material and the reports of other explorers serves to keep one on track, avoiding the pit-falls of self-delusion and inner confusion.

As shown in the previous chapters of this book, symbolic expressions contain great truths that lay hidden, like gold within the earth, waiting to be mined. No one can claim ultimate understanding of the mystery couched in symbols, but in every age there are individuals who wrestle with them to give them an expression that speaks to the soul of the contemporary world. I have tried to find in the symbolism of alchemy a way to understand and give voice to the newly emergent ally experience.

Before turning to some of the alchemical symbols for clarification about the nature of the ally, I would like to remind you of the outline presented in the previous chapters. This blueprint showed that the psychoidal realm exists outside the psyche, which consists of a conscious center known as the ego, and the realm of the unconscious. The ego, as the conscious core of the personality, is the part of the human being that is responsible for engaging with an ally and establishing a relationship and even union with it. But, as indicated earlier, the ally originates in the psychoid realm. Though direct experiences of the psychoid realm are possible, they are rare for individuals starting to work with an ally. Even when psychoidal experiences occur, they are much less common than the psychological experience of inner figures. Most early ally experiences consist of an encounter with an inner ally figure. In the deeper stages of the work, psychic and psychoidal experiences interact and become interlaced, so that the sharp distinction between them is lost. An inner figure that has emerged from the psyche becomes capable of creating psychoidal experiences, and psychoidal energies become embodied in an inner figure. Whether at the beginning or end of the work, however, inner figures are central to the process. Along every step of the way in ally work, one encounters inner figures. To explain more fully the central importance of such inner figures, I will expand on the map previously discussed.

An Image for the Work

In making the attempt to understand a complex and unusual subject such as the work with the ally, it is helpful for you to hold to a central image with which to orient yourself. The whole scope of ally work entails the formation of successive centers and their eventual union.

In a very interesting alchemical text that I have analyzed in greater detail elsewhere,[1] an alchemical writer, Ali Puli, discussed the magical and mystical nature of salt. In his spiritual alchemy, salt plays many roles and symbolizes different aspects of the alchemical process, including the human being and the imagination. In his consideration of salt, he had occasion to speak at length about the center. In fact, the name of his tract is *The Center of Nature Concentrated*. For Ali Puli, salt contains the central power of nature, which, concentrated and focused, creates transmutation. Thus, salt, which is the center, once purified, is the Philosopher's Stone. This is a deep and complicated tract that one could study from several different perspectives. However, I am most interested in Ali's understanding of center.

The first center that Ali discusses lies within the human being. On the sixth day of creation, when God first formed man, "all the dispositions of his [God's] being were shadowed forth through the Mobility of the Divine Spirit, in shape and form in a single and central Light to rule through the brain as Sovereign. This spiritual central seat, God created in man extra to the normal course of Nature, as a new creation, in likeness to Himself, but smaller, for the Honour of God."[2] In other words, God created in man a center made of light, which contained within itself all the aspects and essences of God's own being. In this sense God made man in its own image. The Divine center of man is, however, smaller than the center that God is. This central point within the human psyche is not natural but supernatural, deriving as it does from God. The center of light within man is the inner Divinity, the human-Divine, while the Divine center whose image it is refers to the God-Divine.

The center in alchemy could refer to the center within the human psyche or the transcendent center associated with the Divine. According to the alchemist Gerald Dorn, nothing is more like God than the center, and the center is therefore "an infinite abyss of mysteries." Jung commented on Dorn's conception of the center that it equates "the transcendent centre in man with the God-image. This identification makes it clear why the alchemical symbols for wholeness apply as much to the arcanum in man as to the Deity."[3]

For the alchemists, the center was an eternal and indestructible point that existed at the core of all things, including both the human psyche and God itself. In many ways, the center was the image of God, not only as it existed within the psyche but as it existed in the psychoid world as well. In short, there is a Divine center within and without the soul of man.

The center as it exists within the human being is the Self, or the human-Divine. The center as God is the God-Divine. The goal of ally work is to unite these two centers and to add to this union the ally. The human center Jung called the Self, and the Self, though it exists in latent form, must be manifested through the process Jung called individuation. Ally work relies on individuation for the creation of the first center, but ally work is somewhat different from individuation. If you wish to understand more of the nature of the Self and its creation, you may consult my earlier work, *Jung and the Alchemical Imagination*, as well as the many works of Jung himself. For the purposes of this book, I shall presume that your work of individuation is going on so that the Self is being manifested. I shall discuss later how the ally interacts with the individuation process.

The two centers of divinity exist, one within man and one within the Divine world. Though not opposites in a strict sense, these two centers form two poles of the Divinity. They are split and separated from each other, which is the tragedy of the world. Ally work is the attainment of their union, so that the Divinity is restored to its own wholeness and the centers to their unity. Imagine, therefore, that the human center is on the right side of a page, while the Divine center is on the left. There must be a way to pull them together, and this way is their union within a new center, the ally. The ally is in the center of the page, but at the same time is the page itself. The ally not only becomes the center between the two Divine poles, but also unites them by bringing them into it. I shall return once more to an alchemical image, *Mercurius*, to illustrate this function of the ally.

Mercurius is one of the most interesting of all alchemical motifs. No tract on alchemy neglects a discussion of mercury. For some of the alchemists, mercury was an actual substance of some kind, though rarely mercury as we know it. For many, it was a principle of special power and value, and one main ingredient used to create the Philosopher's Stone.

To begin with, *Mercurius* is a union of opposites and, as such, he is both physical and spiritual. Therefore, Mercury clearly belongs to the psychoid world. He is also the process by which the spiritual is transformed into the material and vice versa. In other words, Mercury refers to the process of transformation itself. Jung elaborates on this idea in a remarkable way. According to Jung, the "alchemists saw him as a divine emanation harmonious with God's own being. The stress they laid on capacity for self-generation, self-transformation, self-reproduction, and self-destruction contradicts the idea that he is a created being. [He is instead] a principle coeternal with God."[4] Mercury is equal with God and yet somehow different from God. As an image of the ally, Mercury depicts both the ally's divinity and yet its differentiation from God.

Part of Mercury's nature as a divine being is to create transformation and another part is to actually be a process of transformation. At the same time, Mercury is not only the process of transformation but also the goal of that transformation. In Jung's terms, Mercury is the process of individuation and the Self that the process creates. He is the "goal of his own transformation."[5]

There is one more important aspect of Mercury. He is a divine entity that creates a process through which he generates himself. The manner in which he does so varies, according to each individual theory of the alchemists, but the creation of Mercury as the stone always involves a union of opposites. Mercury is essential for this union, because he provides the medium in and through which the opposites are united. As Jung wrote, "The coniunctio does not always take the form of a direct union, since it needs—or occurs in—a medium."[6] Mercury is the medium in which the pairs of alchemical opposites are conjoined. In this way, Mercury is the process by which the goal is achieved, it is the goal itself, and it is the medium in which the process occurs. Without a doubt, Mercury was essential for the alchemical opus to succeed.

In much the same way, the ally is necessary for the practical process by which the human and God are united. The ally is the source and director of the process by which this goal is attained; the ally is the goal itself, since it already foreshadows the creation of the Luminous Tree, and the ally is the medium in which the human-Divine and the God-Divine are joined.

Conceiving of the work as the union of two centers—the human-Divine center that is the Self, and the center of the God-Divine—the ally is the medium by which these two centers unite. One could imagine the ally forming a third center, around which the other two unite, thereby creating an axis along which three centers run. Yet the ally is more than the center aligned with the other centers for, as the medium in which union occurs, it contains within itself the other two. The ally enters the Self and the Self of God, uniting them into a whole that is enclosed by and identified with the ally. In this sense, the ally is the goal of the process for when the union of all three is achieved, EO is born.

Thus the objective of the ally work is to heal a split within the Divinity. The ally sets in motion those processes that bring about this healing and unite the human and Divine halves into a whole. From the very beginning of this work until its very end, the ally is key.

Inner Figures

As I mentioned, an individual most often experiences the ally as an inner figure of some kind. Even though the ally originates in the psychoid, it appears in the psyche as an inner figure. To understand the nature of the ally and ally work, we must fully understand the nature of inner figures. To understand inner figures, we first look at the nature of the imagination where these figures are encountered.

Despite the explanations offered by contemporary writers, such as James Hillman and Henry Corbin, most people still misunderstand the *nature* of the imagination. In the Western world, imagination has no real value, except perhaps in an artistic and entertainment sense. As an experience, however, it is less than real, for "real" is defined as only that which the senses can perceive. (Keep in mind that empirical science has ruled the Western mind since the Reformation.) But imagination played a much different role in the worldview of earlier times. Especially during the Renaissance, imagination was of crucial importance in many magical, alchemical, and spiritual practices. As Ioan P. Couliano, in his masterful study of magic in the Renaissance, wrote:

> The revolution in spirit and customs brought about by the
> Reformation led to the total destruction of Renaissance ideals.
> The Renaissance conceived of the natural and social world as

a spiritual organism in which perpetual exchanges of phantasmic messages occurred. That was the principle of magic and of Eros, Eros itself being a form of magic.[7]

The Christian religious leaders, both Catholic and Protestant, in the time of the Reformation, declared war on images and the imagination, and in so doing destroyed the Renaissance ethos, creating the contemporary materialistic and anti-spiritual attitude of science. Couliano discussed in great detail the theory of imagination that was central to the Renaissance and its belief in magic. I will not discuss that theory at this time, but refer interested readers to his book. I do, however, wish to present the view of imagination that many alchemists held, a view that related them to all the magical and occult practices of their time. An alchemist of the 17th century, Oswald Croll, wrote:

> By the help of Imagination all magical operations and all wonderful things are done through the natural in born faith, by which we are at peace with the very spirits themselves. The Imagination worketh in Man like the sun, or as the bodily sun worketh without an instrument upon the subject burning it to coals and ashes, so the incorporeal cogitation of man worketh on the subject, by the spirit only as with a visible instrument; what the visible body doth that also doth the invisible body.[8]

In other words, imagination has the power to create material changes without use of a physical instrument, just as the Sun can burn an object to ashes without ever touching it. Like the rays of the Sun, the powers of the imagination act on the "subject," the alchemical substance, to create transformations within it. Croll, like many other alchemists, believed that the true power of transmutation lay not in physical processes alone, but in the uncanny power of the imagination. It was the imagination, skillfully employed by the alchemists, that could cause lead to change into gold, or produce elixirs, or even generate the wished-for Philosopher's Stone.

Imagination was also the means by which union with the Divine was achieved. Croll wrote that "many also by their intent Imagination, without distrust of their weakness, by a constant and most firm faith toward God, by a mind lifted up most high, by infallible hope, constant and most ardent prayers, have so prevailed that on a sudden they have become the Temples of the Living God."⁹

Croll was not alone in his belief in the powers of the imagination. There are many alchemists writing in that period, but Croll's words clearly express the alchemical view of imagination, a view that Jung most certainly knew and related to in his own research. So profound did Jung find imagination's role in alchemy that he wrote, "The *imaginatio*, as the alchemists understand it, is, in truth, a key that opens the door to the secret of the opus."¹⁰ According to the alchemists, imagination had several different functions. It was instrumental in gaining wisdom and the required knowledge to perform alchemy, for many of the alchemists believed the secrets of their work could only be conveyed through revelation, either from God directly or from their good genius. Moreover, as we have just seen, imagination was the secret of all magical works, and the means by which the alchemists directly affected the material components within their retort. Imagination was the means of gaining wisdom, and the means by which transformation was created.

In all these ways, the alchemical esoteric tradition developed the concept of imagination.

One of Jung's greatest achievements was to rediscover the importance of the imagination. One of the central tenets of Jung's theory is that imaginative encounter with the unconscious is instrumental in the creation of the inner Self, and promotes every aspect of the individuation process. He developed a technique through which one could produce imaginal encounters with the unconscious. Using this technique, which he termed "active imagination," the individual is able to encounter inner figures of every type and, working through them, create a profound psychological transformation. Active imagination is a process through which the ego is able to encounter the unconscious in a waking state. Through active imagination, the ego is able to engage the inner figures that populate our dream life. Learning the technique of active imagination requires effort, but one who masters it is able to enter the inner world at will. I shall discuss in greater detail the practice of active imagination in the next chapter.

But it is Croll's profound statement that imagination makes one a temple of the Living God that most concerns us. Ally work transforms one into such a temple, and the ally is the Divine spirit that resides within it. Ally work begins with the discovery of the ally as an inner figure and progresses to the point at which the ally becomes the incarnation of God, or what in earlier chapters was termed the Luminous Tree.

So the ally is an inner figure, but what exactly is an inner figure? In his study of the spirit, Jung came to the conclusion that spirit possessed spontaneous movement and activity. The spirit is free to do and create as it will, and is free of the control of the ego, the conscious part of the personality. The ego can experience the spirit, but not dictate to it. The second attribute of spirit, according to Jung, is the capacity to spontaneously produce images, and the third attribute is the "sovereign manipulation of these images."[11] Experientially, every human being encounters the spirit in his or her dreams, for the images that populate their dreams derive from the spirit. Not only the images themselves, but all that they do in the dreams are a reflection of spirit. In this sense, the ego does not make up dreams; rather, it experiences them as they unfold through the spontaneous manifestation of the spirit.

The spirit, as it relates to the unconscious and all its contents, has the capacity to produce images and experiences related to those images. Every part of the unconscious, whether it is complex or archetype, can appear as an image. Every inner figure is a personification of a part of the unconscious. Every inner figure possesses spirit, or the capacity to express itself autonomously, and thus the inner figure is the self-portrayal of an unconscious content.

Let us take a dream as a simple example. We all have dreams every night that are made up of symbols. In this dream, a man unlocks his basement door and walks down a long flight of steps. When he reaches the bottom he comes to a door that is locked. Looking around on the floor, he discovers a key that opens the door. As he opens it, a beautiful woman in a blue gown smiles and beckons him to enter. Now, all the contents of this dream are images. The door, the lock, the key, the flight of stairs are all symbolic and significant expressions. The young woman, however, is a living being who, by waving at the man, is relating to his dream ego. The young woman is an inner figure. She personifies some aspect of the dreamer's own feminine nature. If the dreamer, on waking, were to continue the dream through active imagination he would proceed to relate to the young woman and ideally have a conversation with her. Through one or many such active imagination experiences he can learn about his own feminine nature and in fact even transform it. An image that is alive and capable of relating to the conscious personality is an inner figure.

Often the inner figure is perceived as a clear image, such as the image of the young woman mentioned above. However, not all individuals experience personifications in the same way. Some are able to visualize clearly, and form the image of the young woman in their mind. They can see her features distinctly and will notice the color of her hair or of her eyes. Other people are not able to visualize so distinctly, but may *hear* things more easily. They experience the inner figure as a voice talking with them. Still others can neither see nor hear the imaginal realm, but are able to feel, sometimes with a direct knowing of what the inner figure is communicating. Thus, an inner figure may appear as a perceptible image, a voice, or a feeling. In all these different cases, however, the individual is aware of the presence of a personality within the imaginal realm that is communicating with him or her. Just how they receive the communication is not so important.

In teaching someone to work with inner figures I emphasize the person's talent rather than their weakness. One who can visualize well should use that modality, while one who hears more lucidly should dialogue. Once students have gained a certain facility in dealing with inner figures, I encourage them to develop the modality with which they are less adept. If you have visualized an inner figure well, you should next try to talk with it. If you are successful in doing so, you should next attempt to feel the inner figure deeply. In time, you will come to experience the inner figure in several different ways. Therefore, when I say that some aspect of the unconscious personifies itself as an inner figure, I do not always mean an image has been formed. The unconscious can express itself equally as well in words and in feelings. Yet the map that we have constructed in this book goes beyond the psyche and the unconscious to include the psychoid realm and those powers that inhabit it.

Inner figures may in fact embody the psychoid as well as contents of the unconscious. Such inner figures may express themselves in a visual image, or speak, or create feeling states. In this regard, they resemble inner figures that embody the unconscious. However, there are differences in the experiences that they engender. The visual images they create are often more intense and sometimes are perceptible even when one has one's eyes open. Sometimes they are accompanied with intense colors and bright lights, and they seem more autonomous than other inner figures. If one is relating to a psychoidal figure verbally, one discovers that often their words create experiences. The words do not just communicate information but also actually produce the results they are speaking of. With an inner figure that is not psychoidal, dialogue resembles dialogue with another person. The inner figure may describe, for example, a certain ecstatic state and the ego learns something of its nature. But if a psychoidal figure describes an ecstatic state, the ego enters that state and experiences it. There are differences at the level of feeling as well. Our language is not well suited for explaining such different feeling states, but as a rough approximation, I might state that psychoidal figures generate more profound feelings than other figures. The feelings are often ecstatic, and the entity creating them feels alien to the ego. It is therefore possible to discriminate between psychic and psychoidal inner figures by the nature of the experiences that they create.

Hundreds of years before Jung, a Sufi Islamic mystic explored the nature of the imaginal world and the figures that inhabit it. This master, Ibn 'Arabi, wrote that the imagination was intermediary between the world of human life and the Divine Reality. Events from the ordinary human world could appear as images in the imaginal realm. This certainly occurs in dream life, where our daily experiences are represented in symbolic terms. However, the beings from the higher Divine world may also present themselves in the imagination. The Divinity manifests, along with spirits, in the intermediate world. When a messenger or a being from the higher world wishes to communicate with a human being, it does so through the imagination. Ibn 'Arabi wrote that one way the spirits communicate is to take on form and become inner figures. Moreover, he assures us that the inner figure is identical with the spiritual being who appears in that form:

> But the form is not other than the spiritual being itself; on the contrary, it is identical with it, even if it is found in a thousand places, or in all places, and is diverse in shape.[12]

The spiritual beings of the psychoid realm take on form within the imagination, and though the form is an inner experience, it is identical with the psychoidal being who adopts it. A psychoidal sensation connects an individual with a force, being or energy that feels "other" than the experiencer. It feels as if it were coming from outside oneself and does not feel inward at all. A client was once meditating when she entered a state in which she could not move. Fully awake, she found herself paralyzed.

This state of paralysis is not uncommon in people on the threshold of a psychoid experience. As she lay unable to move, she felt what she thought was a cat jump on the bed and begin to lick her face. After a short time the cat began to speak, telling her it loved her and needed her company. It then left and she felt herself able to move again.

In this typical psychoid experience, an individual experiences an altered state of some kind, here, paralysis. An entity or energy then enters one's environment and begins an interaction of some sort. In the situation just described, the woman sensed that the entity was a cat, though she never saw a cat or any other image for that matter. The communication occurred here with words and sensations that conveyed great feeling.

Such experiences are infrequent. You certainly cannot count on them occurring often in the beginning of ally work, so if you were to rely on such experiences to form a relationship with the ally, the process would be impossibly slow. The alternative method is to do active imagination with an inner figure that personifies the psychoid entity that first appeared. In this example, the ally already felt like a cat, so that the woman could continue to relate to her ally by doing active imagination with the inner figure of the cat. Since the inner figure and the psychoid cat are so closely related as to be identical, when the woman does active imagination with the inner figure of the cat she is also directly relating to the entity personified by that figure.

At the beginning, such inner figures are not really psychoidal, but only point to the psychoid. As the work with the ally progresses, the ally figure embodies more and more of the psychoidal ally, and the figure begins to generate experiences of greater depth and profundity.

However, a psychoidal entity may personify as a figure at any time and can affect the person in profound ways. Ally work attempts to unite a psychic inner figure with a psychoidal entity, in this way uniting psyche and psychoid.

Thus, the inner figure may personify some aspect of the unconscious, such as an archetype, or it may, in fact, embody a psychoidal spirit, such as the ally. Though the ally as a psychoidal being has its own life in the psychoid, it is approximately identical to the image that appears within the imagination. This is a crucial statement for ally work, for it means that working in the imaginal realm with the inner figure of the ally connects one with the psychoidal entity that is personified in the figure. Union with the figure is union with the ally. Transformation of the figure is transformation of the ally. The inner figure is therefore the key to all ally work.

In the next chapter I shall demonstrate the ways in which the inner figure undergoes the transformation through which it embodies more and more of the psychoidal entity that is the ally. The further the work progresses, the more profound are the affects created by the inner figure. Yet even at the beginning of the work, the inner figure personifies, to one degree or another, one's ally.

Jung described his own interaction with an inner figure in his autobiography when he wrote of his experience of *Philemon*. His description of this experience provides a model for understanding the nature of such events:

> Philemon and other figures of my fantasies brought home to
> me the crucial insight that there are things in the psyche which

I do not produce, but which produce themselves and have their own life. Philemon represented a force which was not myself. In my fantasies I held conversations with him, and he said things which I had not consciously thought. For I observed clearly that it was he who spoke, not I. . . . He confronted me in an objective manner, and I understood that there is something in me which can say things that I do not know and do not intend, things which may even be directed against me . . . Philemon . . . was a mysterious figure to me. At times he seemed quite real, as if he were a living personality.[13]

Inner figures, such as Philemon, are experienced in the imaginal realm. They feel real to the experiencer, and emanate a personality as well as a living presence. Not everyone will experience a figure as profound as Philemon, but everyone can experience an inner figure that seems alive and related to him or her. Jung not only sensed Philemon's presence, he engaged in dialogues with him. Inner figures may talk or in some manner communicate with an individual, and in this communication lies one of the most extraordinary ways of relating to them. They can present information or penetrating insights, or just chat. In the communication and exchange with them, the ego discovers the reality of the imaginal world. As Jung said, the inner figures appear as if they were objective, possessed of autonomy and reality. This is true of all inner figures, but the more you work with them, the more alive they become. If the inner figure is related to the psychoid, its autonomy and "otherness" become strikingly part of any experience you have of them.

Without subjective experience of such encounters, you may not realize the difference between figures that relate to the psychoid and those that do not. After all, both are inner figures. However, with practice, you can begin to differentiate between encounters with inner figures of a psychoidal nature and those that personify unconscious forces or contents. Active imagination with the inner figure relates you to the entity that creates that figure. If that entity belongs to the unconscious, the nature of the encounter, however profound it may be, is psychic and imaginal. It typically occurs with eyes closed and attention diverted within. If the entity is of the psychoid realm, the encounter not only includes this inner, imaginal sense but has psychoidal affects as well. Such affects might include a major shift of consciousness into an altered state, a shift in bodily state, such as a healing experience, or production of energy or heat within the body. In such cases, the inner image creates a sense or feel of another that appears to be outside you, outside your own inner world. Your eyes may be open, and you may be gazing on the inner figure manifesting energy in the room, or producing a clear sense of energy interactions. This may be a difficult notion to grasp, but in your *feeling*, the inner figure connected to the psychoid appears to be different from an inner figure that is not psychoid.

The ally might first appear in a dream as "magical animal," or a numinous, angelic being. Typically, the figure will express its deep love for the individual, and the individual will experience this love. The dreamer often has the sense of being seen or met for the first time in his life. There is a distinct bonding quality to the dream, and the perception that one has met an inner lover and friend. If the individual continues to work with the inner figure in a waking state, the relationship develops.

Since the inner figure is a resident of the imagination, cultivating the relationship with it requires that the individual enter the imaginal realm. In one of his most important contributions, Jung developed a technique by which this may be accomplished. He termed this practice active imagination, and through it an individual may, while fully awake and conscious, experience the imaginal figures. It is important to keep in mind that working with an inner figure is an actual practice that one can adopt, and through such an exercise an individual can experience the reality of the ally for him- or herself.

The alchemists were aware of such inner figures, and they experienced them in imaginal encounters and presented them symbolically in their pictures and writings. They termed one in particular the "genius." The encounters between the alchemist and the genius form a fascinating part of alchemy and have much to teach us about the nature of the ally and the ally relationship.

The Genius

The origins of the concept of the genius, and its related notion, the *daemon*, lie in ancient Greek thought. In alchemy, the genius was related to active imagination. Ruland, who compiled a lexicon of alchemical terms, defined meditation as the "name of an Internal Talk of one person with another who is invisible, as in the invocation of the Deity, or communion with one's self, or with one's good angel."[14] This good angel is the same as the genius, and in fact the earlier notion of genius and daemon had a great impact on the Christian view of angelic beings. The genius is invisible, which marks it as a spirit. Moreover, Ruland differentiates three types of beings with whom one may engage in dialogue:

the Deity, the self, and the good angel. If you recall the model we explored in the previous chapter, which presented the human-Divine, the God-Divine, and the ally, you can see that Ruland's differentiation is very similar. The communion with one's Self would correspond to working with the human-Divine, while the invocation of the Deity would characterize experiencing the God-Divine. The genius is not the Self, nor is it the Divinity. It is a third category of spiritual being, which we have referred to as the ally.

Active Imagination and the Genius

Jung found Ruland's definition of meditation interesting. He thought that it proved convincingly that meditation did not mean mere cogitation, but an active inner dialogue with "the answering voice of the other in ourselves." The genius is therefore an inner figure with whom one can dialogue and thereby form what Jung called "a living relationship."[15]

In a living relationship, both partners are acutely aware of each other. The ego, or human partner, pays attention to and consults the inner figure of the genius, and the genius communicates through word and image with the ego. Both partners are vitally engaged, and both respect the other's independence. All important decisions, all life changes are taken by the two partners together, with no denial or repression of either. Out of this on-going engagement between the two emerges not only a new way of living but also a loving bond that unites them more deeply than ever before.

A person who wishes to form a relationship with an ally must at some point learn active imagination. This technique for contacting inner figures, though rediscovered by Jung, is ancient. Using this technique, one enters the imaginal world while fully awake and interacts with the denizens of that reality. One of the most important of such experiences is dialogue, for conversing with inner figures has many profound effects. It permits the exchange of information between the ego and the inner figure, helps create a relationship between the two, and sets in motion processes that will both transform and unite them. But whether one dialogues, sees, or simply feels, active imagination is essential to the formation of a living and loving relationship with the genius.

Active imagination thus creates the living relationship that Jung mentions, and nothing is more important in working with the genius. The genius becomes not only a guide or source of information, but an inner friend and companion. Walking and talking with this friend in the imaginal world is a great joy, informative, and stimulating. One does not always engage the ally or genius in deep spiritual work, for at times the active imagination connection with it is light and playful. One can spend many hours lying together by a stream, or simply learning how the other "feels." Nevertheless, it also proves to be a source of much knowledge and necessary insight.

The alchemists imagined that interacting with the genius would provide them with the information that they sought in their work. There were so many unknowns and imponderables in alchemy that many sought Divine inspiration. One way they experienced such insights and openings was through active imagination. In his commentary on the writings of Basil Valentine, Theodore Kirkringius wrote that the alchemists knew how important Divine help was in the work and "how often those things which he long sought and could not find have been imparted to him a moment, and as it were infused from above, or dictated by some good

Genius."[16] The genius then conveys not just information, but knowledge, and is associated with the Divine Wisdom itself. Notice that Kirkringius describes the exchange of information as an infusion. The genius communicates not only with words, but also in direct transmission of knowledge. In whatever way it communicates, however, the experience is often accompanied with a certainty of knowing. It is this certainty that most characterizes the encounter with the genius.

Like the alchemist, the contemporary individual who struggles to individuate faces many difficult problems and unknown quantities. I have worked analytically with people for over twenty-five years and know full well how hard it is to create inner change, or to become the person each of us is meant to be. Our own complexes sneak up on us when least expected. Other people's projections interfere with our growth and the mysterious unknown nature of the inner world is both daunting and inhibiting. Imagine, if you will, embarking on this difficult journey, one that might last all your life. Imagine doing it alone, with no guide and no inner helper. Imagine that you must discover everything you need to understand yourself—the world, and the unconscious—all by yourself. It is not only a frightening proposition, it is next to impossible to accomplish. Of course, you can enter analysis and receive help in that way, and you can read and study, as well as seek out a community of like-minded friends. But none of these, even combined, makes as big an impact as having an inner spirit who can teach, guide, and encourage, no matter what hardships must be endured.

Being in analysis or therapy is as essential as having friends with whom you can share your experiences. But no matter how profound these aids are, the inner companion so loves you and feels so supportive, that its words and teachings are in themselves transformative. When I am analyzing a person who has an image of the genius, I encourage him or her to dialogue with that figure whenever possible. I encourage such a person to follow the advice of the genius almost without exception, and I see my job as simply encouraging the relationship that is unfolding between the ego and the genius. I wish to be clear that I am not minimizing the need for an outer guide, teacher or analyst. Even with an ally, having some real person to talk with is very important. However, I have often been struck by the fact that a person who has an ally is much more prepared and better able to face the challenges of individuation than one who does not, even if both are in analysis.

When faced with a complex, for example, the ego may turn to the genius for insight and information. When in a complex, which is a part of the personal unconscious that has its own feeling state and can take over the ego, the ego often feels overwhelmed by emotions and ideas that are most disturbing and often paralyzing. One may remain in such a state until the emotions contained within a complex wear themselves out or some intervention is made. This intervention may come from within or from without but turning to the ally for help is always a good idea. For the genius does more than give good advice or present information; it can actually alter the psychological state of the person with whom it is relating. Not always, but often, a dialogue or encounter with the genius produces a shift in the mood or psychological state. Especially if one begins dialoguing while in the grips of a complex, the meeting with the genius may pull one out of that state and restore one to inner equilibrium. The feelings produced by the genius are of equal importance to the knowledge it conveys.

THE GENIUS AS TEACHER

The alchemists struggled to give expression to the powerful ways in which the genius taught, and more than one had occasion to compare its power in this regard to the power of God. For example, one alchemist wrote, "A Physician should be born out of the Light of Grace and Nature of the inward and invisible Man, the internal Angel, the Light of Nature, which like a Doctor teacheth and instructeth men, as the Holy Spirit taught the Apostles in fiery tongues."[17] The internal angel, or the genius, is likened to the Holy Spirit and the intensity of its communication with the fire of the Pentecost. Moreover, it is this inner teaching that makes a man skilled and wise, rather than what he learns from books or from others. This was a theme that the alchemists emphasized over and over again: true wisdom comes from the teaching of the inner spirit. The genius is the source of a wisdom that is not intellectual but rather experiential. The teachings of the inner spirit are often not even in words, or the words only carry the outer husk of the message: a message that is felt rather than thought.

Writing in a letter that he never expected to be published, the alchemist George Starkey clearly reveals the felt sense of the encounter with the genius. After spending hours in hard work, Starkey fell asleep and had the following dream:

> Behold! I seemed intent on my work, and a man appeared, entering the laboratory, at whose arrival I was stupefied. But he greeted me and said, "May God support our labors." When I heard this, realizing that he had mentioned God [and so was not of the Devil], I asked who he was, and he responded that

he was my Eugenius. I asked whether there were such creatures. He responded that there were. . . . Finally I asked him what the alkahest of Paracelsus and Helmont was, and he responded that they used salt, sulfur and an alkalized body, and though this response was more obscure than Paracelsus himself, yet with the response an ineffable light entered my mind, so that I fully understood. Marveling at this, I said to him, "Behold! Your words are veiled, as it were by fog, and yet they are fundamentally true." He said, "This is so necessarily, for the things said by one's Eugenius are all certain."[18]

The genius may use words, but often when it speaks it creates an experience by which something is known directly, though the words themselves may be most obscure. The inner figure in the dream speaks directly from the source, for it is the genius itself that is communicating. Not only does it reveal the mystery Starkey sought, it creates an experience of light and, therefore, of enlightenment. Moreover, it assures Starkey that beings such as the genius are real, and that they speak certain truth. The ally or genius does not lie, it does not confuse or trick; it speaks that which is most certain and true. And when it speaks, it creates not just words, but experiences.

Words are powerful instruments in the spiritual life. Several traditions view certain language as holy, such as Hebrew and Sanskrit, and mystics believe that such languages contain power over and above the linguistic usage of the word. Words have affects and are used in meditations and mantras, as well as in magical rites. Mystics such as Abraham ben Samuel Abulafia taught that contemplation of letters and words led to prophecy and direct insight into the nature of God. Such mystics discovered the felt dimension of language, and nowhere is this more clearly experienced than in encounters with the genius. The words spoken by the other, when we engage in active imagination, simultaneously communicate and create, so that the teaching becomes the experience of what is taught. This does not always happen, but it does happen with increasing regularity, the deeper the relationship with the genius. Starkey experienced this felt power of language in his dream, and we may experience it in active imagination work with the inner figure of the genius.

THE GENIUS AND THE SELF

Not only is the genius a teacher and creator of experience, it is closely related to the nature of our Self. It can reveal our true character and the depth of our uniqueness. The discovery of the genius often reveals the purpose of our life. The 16th-century magician Cornelius Agrippa had a great influence on the alchemists of his time. He wrote that the genius prompts an individual to follow a true path and give full expression to his or her inner nature. He recommended looking back at our life and observing where the "instinct of our nature" and the inner heavens led us to. If we were perfectly to follow our inner promptings and take note of them, we would be in harmony with the Self and living what Jung called our personal myth. The genius inclines us to lead such a life, for these inner promptings are "without all doubt the persuasions of a Genius which is given to everyone from their birth, leading, and persuading us to that whither the star thereof inclines us to."[19]

In Agrippa's view, there is an inner star that creates our own unique destiny and urges us to live a life based on whom we really are; this inner

star is the genius. Jung, too, believed that every human being had a personal myth, a reason to be alive, and a call to follow. We are, each of us,
unique in some way, and to find our uniqueness and express it is instrumental in creating psychological health. A life based on our true nature,
on our own feelings and perceptions, is a healthy life. All too often,
however, we live as others want us to live, or as we think we are supposed
to live. Living outside ourselves, we create neurosis and fear, insecurity
and anxiety, as we seek to please the incessant demands of a voice other
than our own. To find our own truth is an essential but rarely-accom-
plished task.

We can learn about ourselves through the encounter with the ally,
who will also reveal the things that bring joy and fulfillment into our
lives. The genius knows us, mirrors us and spurs us on to know ourselves. In this way, it aids in the formation of the Self and supports the
individuation process in all its manifestations. That which it teaches is
always true for the person being taught. It never imposes ideas or ideals
from a source not in harmony with the inner self. The genius can be
demanding, but it never demands more than this: that we struggle to be
truly ourselves and that we enter into relationship with it as free and
whole beings. Rather than urge submission or obedience, it demands
equality and partnership.

Jung realized that part of the personal myth included a connection
with the Divine. He was intensely concerned with the struggle between
the individual and the mass, for he feared that the individual, the greatest miracle of life, would be lost to mass consciousness and society. The
greatest protection against submersion in the mass is to know oneself,
but it is equally important to know the Divine. The person who is

anchored in an inner connection to the Divine is rooted in a source so powerful that it protects him or her from being swept away by mass consciousness of any kind. If he or she has an experience of the numinous, no other person, no other movement or teaching, can ever take that experience away. The inner transcendent experience grounds a person in her own truth and protects her from persuasions of the mass.

In my early twenties, I experienced a visitation of the ally, which came with great love and purpose. I knew nothing about psychology or spirituality, and was both elated and frightened by my experience. Not knowing any better, I shared something of its nature with friends and family, all of who, as with one voice, urged me to give up such things and get on with my life. I was in graduate school and had planned the next four years. Part of me wanted nothing more than to follow such good advice, but the nature of my ally experiences precluded my doing so. I could not ignore the reality and depth of what I had experienced, and though it took me years to understand the message of the genius, I could deny neither its power nor its imperative that I know myself and live my own life. These experiences protected me from the well-meaning advice of those around me and I am thankful to this day that I trusted my genius and not my friends. Collective pressure to conform can be much harsher than what I experienced, for difference is rarely tolerated. As Jung knew, feeling a direct and intimate personal relationship with God shields one from this pressure. The numinosity and bliss of spiritual knowledge allows us to stand firmly in our own truth without having to leave the world or to make others wrong.

The genius not only reveals the nature of our self, it provides a personal experience of the Divine. In fact, it is the means by which we can first experience the human-Divine core within. Through the relationship with the genius, we encounter Divine truth, which is the essential part of the personal myth, and we garner the strength to live that myth. Although the struggle to be ourself is not easy, it leads to a fuller and richer life. Another magician of the Renaissance, Marsilio Ficinio, wrote that "whoever discovers his own genius . . . will thus find his own natural work, and at the same time he will find his own star and daemon. Following these beginnings he will do well and live happily.[20]

The genius can teach an individual not only about the secrets of life, but about his or her own nature and the characteristics of one's personal myth. There is no greater wisdom than self-knowledge, especially knowledge that includes not only who a person is, but also what they are to do with their life. Knowing oneself and living one's myth are the ingredients for a joyful, albeit challenging life.

Oswald Croll wrote about the nature of the genius as well, from several different perspectives, all of which are significant. To begin with, he called the genius "our private angel . . . the familiar homunculus."[21] That the genius might be related to a private angel is not surprising, but if we combine this notion with some of the ideas already discussed, a fuller picture emerges. The genius is an angelic or spiritual being and there is a genius for every human being. In this sense, the genius is one's own private spiritual entity. An inner figure personifies and embodies this private entity, so that each person may find his own angel through encounter with an inner figure. As indicated, the genius not only is specific to each person, it knows that person intimately and reflects his or her own unique nature. In being private to a person, the genius actually participates and mirrors that person's uniqueness.

Though there are many commonalties in the experience of the ally, each individual experiences his genius in ways unique only to him. This is one hallmark of working with a genius, for there is always a feel about the experience that is special. Though I may teach others about their genius and give them ideas about how to work with it, I can never tell them what it will teach or how it will feel. I can never indoctrinate them into a dogma that I have created, for each genius will teach them truths and mysteries in unique and highly personal ways. I can only point the way, hoping that the individual will discover his or her own special truth.

THE GENIUS AND THE FILIUS

It is necessary, here, to discuss the homunculus to further understand Croll's viewpoint of the genius. Again, I will restrict myself to the alchemical understanding of this entity. Paracelsus, who had a great influence on Croll, wrote most about the homunculus. Paracelsus was a very important figure in the development of alchemy and in the history of medicine, but he was also interested in magic and mysticism. For him, the homunculus was a magical entity that was very small and that could be created through alchemical efforts. If the alchemist took human semen and allowed it to putrefy in a sealed vessel for 40 days, it would, at the end of that time, become agitated and begin to move. Fed human blood for another 40 weeks, it would become a living baby, only much smaller than a human baby. Because it was created in this magical way, it possessed great wisdom and power. Paracelsus grew ecstatic as he described it, calling it "one of the greatest secrets which God has revealed to mortal and fallible man. It is a miracle and marvel of God, and arcanum above all arcana."[22] From it may be produced other magical beings, such as pygmies and giants, "who are the instruments of great things, who get great victories over their enemies, and know all secret and hidden matters."[23] The homunculi look like men, but they are really spirits.

The homunculus is clearly a very powerful magical being. It is a spirit formed in a tiny human body, and it not only has the knowledge of great mysteries, it has a great power that it can lend to the alchemist. It is also the incarnation of the alchemical enterprise, for being created by the alchemical work, "art is incorporated in [it]."[24] Jung explains that this strange being corresponds to the inner spiritual being, the *lapis* or the *filius*. In other words, the homunculus is no other than the *filius philosophorum*, or the Philosopher's Stone, itself.[25]

As we shall soon see, clearly Croll equates the genius or the homunculus with the goal of the alchemical work. Moreover, the homunculus appears in such alchemical writings as *The Chemical Wedding of Christian Rosenkreutz*, as the newly formed king and queen that alchemy has brought back from death. The genius is equated with the homunculus, which in turn is equated to the filius. In *Jung and the Alchemical Imagination*, I demonstrated that the *filius* is in fact another symbol for the ally,[26] so it is not surprising to see genius and *filius* compared in this way. But the *filius* refers to the end of the work, to the product that the transformations of alchemy produce, while the genius, on the other hand, is always present and able to guide the alchemist from the very beginning of his work. Still, the equation of the genius with the *filius* is of great significance, for it establishes the fact that the genius, though present from the start, is transformed to become the Philosopher's Stone. It does not remain the same, but through alchemical processes becomes far different from what it was at the start. The genius is the ally as it appears before the work is accomplished. The *filius* would be the final state of the ally when its work has been accomplished. The ally's human partner transforms the genius, by paying attention to it, into the filius. Though clearly one entity, the ally experiences transformation at different stages as it evolves with its partner. I shall explain the nature of these changes in greater detail during later discussions of the stages of the ally work.

Croll speaks of the genius in other ways that connect it to the *filius.* He calls it "the light of nature." Jung wrote that light is "the central mystery of alchemy. Almost always it is personified as the filius, or mentioned as one of his outstanding attributes."[27] Both the genius and the *filius* are then related to light, the central mystery of alchemy. Once more, Croll's attributions relate the genius to the end product of the alchemical work and the very core mysteries of alchemy.

The Genius and Light

Light is a major symbol found in mysticism and religion the world over. It is beyond the scope of this chapter to examine all the meanings of light, but aspects of its symbolism clarify the nature of the genius. If the genius is the light of nature, then we must examine this later image to learn more about the genius.

Light is almost universally connected with spirit. Spiritual forces and beings are often experienced as pure light. They glow with radiance or possess a halo of light. To be enlightened is to be filled with spiritual wisdom and power. In a great many spiritual traditions, light is associated with the Divinity itself, or with parts of the divinity. In shamanism, for example, light is a central part of the inner experience of the shaman. Rasmussin, a student of shamanism, wrote that the shaman's empowerment consisted of "a mysterious light which the shaman suddenly feels in his body, inside his head, within the brain, an inexplicable searchlight, a luminous fire, which enables him to see in the dark both literally and metaphorically speaking. . . . Nothing is hidden from him any longer; not only can he see things far, far away, but also he can discover souls, stolen souls."[28]

For the Sufi mystics of Islam, who were often great alchemists as well, light was of great importance. The goal of the mystic work was to discover and liberate the man of light, who is a captive in the darkness of forgetfulness. The man of light is the self of the mystic, but there is another man of light. The second man of light is twin to the first, and is a guide and a "heavenly entity, the philosopher's Angel, conjoined with his star, which rules him and opens the door of wisdom for him, detaches from what is difficult, reveals to him what is right, in sleeping as in waking."[29] The Angel is, of course, identical to the genius, and in Sufi theory embodies Divine light and wisdom. It is the twin of the self and guides the man of light to the Divinity.

In alchemy as well, light is, in Jung's words, a central mystery. In the alchemy of Isaac Newton, for example, light "represented the power of God to activate or reactivate lifeless matter."[30] The light of nature illuminates all the mysteries of life, and though some alchemists like Paracelsus are careful to distinguish it from the supernatural light of Christ, it nevertheless reveals all things. Jung explains that the light of nature is "the source of mystical knowledge second only to the holy revelation of the Scriptures."[31]

The light of nature is the embodiment of inner wisdom and the Divine power that manifests itself in creation. If the genius, like the *fil-*

ius, is equated with this light, it means that as an inner figure it personifies spiritual power and wisdom. It knows the secrets of nature and the supernatural and it understands the mysteries of transformation. If we think of alchemy as the science of transformation, the genius holds the keys to that science. It reveals the path and the mysteries that surround that path, and allows the aspirant to gain self-knowledge and move beyond the Self to encounter the psychoidal Divine. As the Sufi man of light has his or her twin of light that guides him or her to union with God, the alchemist has the genius that leads to the formation of the Philosopher's Stone, the symbol of human and Divine union.

As a figure of light, however, the genius not only leads to the Divine and its experience, but also is in itself a divinity of some kind. Though differentiated from the Divine-Divine, the ally is a Divinity in its own right. It partakes of the Divine essence and personifies it as a helping and guiding figure. In fact, if the ally were not Divine itself, it would be hard to imagine that it could unite the other two aspects of divinity, the human-Divine and the God-Divine. Rather than simply existing as an intermediate being, the ally is an aspect of the Divine totality. As genius, it appears with the light of Divinity and illuminates the Divine inner self of that person. Yet it also joins with the Divine-Divine, shining with the light of its own Divine nature.

The Genius and the Imagination

Croll is not done with his discussion of the genius. The next part of his description reveals the depths of the genius' nature and some of the secrets of working with it:

> [The genius] is also called the Imagination, which encloseth all
> the astras, and is indeed all the astras or Stars and holdeth the
> same course, Nature and power with Heaven . . . Now the
> astras or stars . . . are nothing else but the virtues or powers of
> the angells. The angells which live only upon the vision of God,
> are the created Wisdom of God. Hence he that knows God
> knows the astras also.[32]

The genius is the equivalent of imagination, which contains all the stars
or angels—personifications of the power and wisdom of God. As such,
the genius is the inner figure that personifies imagination's powers. These
powers and virtues are the direct manifestation of the Divine.

One way of thinking about alchemy is to envision it as an attempt
to incarnate spiritual powers within a material form. Inner alchemy,
which is concerned with the direct conscious experience of cosmic
forces, seeks to embody the powers of the archetypes as well as psychoidal spirits in the Philosopher's Stone. The genius is the guide that,
through its Divine wisdom, leads the adept to the sought-for treasure;
the genius is the very treasure being sought and the means by which the
treasure is found. As the personification of imagination, the inner figure of the genius makes available to its human partner the wisdom and
powers of the imaginative worlds and the denizens that inhabit them.
These inhabitants include archetypal inner figures and psychoidal spiritual powers. Through the work with its human partner, the genius
comes to include and integrate all these diverse powers, uniting them
within itself in a harmonious, albeit complex, fashion.

Ally work begins with the creation of a relationship with the ally or genius. The individual embarking on ally work discovers an inner partner who loves him and teaches him the secrets of self-nature, as well as the mysteries of the Divine world. At the same time, the partner embodies a great imaginative power, capable of creating experiences of all kinds. It generates dialogues, visions, and revelations and puts at its partner's disposal the *astra*, or angelic powers, that are the closest thing to the Divine. Through these visions, the ally or genius leads its partner to the direct encounter with the God-Divine and establishes a union between them. Finally, as the imaginative power, the genius unites the human-Divine and the God-Divine and, entering the union itself, creates the Philosopher's Stone, the *filius philosophorum*. The Philosopher's Stone is the alchemical equivalent of the Luminous Tree. In this way, the genius is the guide on the path, the instrument by which the goal is accomplished, and the goal itself. For as it transforms from genius to *filius*, the Philosopher's Stone comes into being.

The one element seemingly missing from the alchemical account of the ally is love. The contemporary experience of the genius is characterized by a deep and abiding love that is both healing and transformative. The ally does not promise power or wisdom, but love and union. It brings wisdom and power in the wake of love, but love remains its principal gift. It is true that love is not always mentioned by the alchemists, but they did not ignore it entirely either. For example, one alchemist titles the *filius* the "love-child" or the "child of love."[33] There are other references to love in alchemy, and, as in most Renaissance thinking, Eros is a principle element in the magical work that the alchemists perform.

Regardless of how it was for the alchemists of the past, today the ally experience is one of love. I have not met a single individual who has had an ally experience who did not describe it in terms of love. Perhaps because our culture has mastered technology and thereby produced powers and benefits that an alchemist could only dream of, the emphasis on power has shifted. The contemporary individual typically has many creature comforts and is assured of a healthy and long life. The needs for survival are not usually pressing. Living in a world such as ours, we are able to turn to what is most missing from our lives: relationship with the Divine. The need to place ourselves in right relationship with God is met by encountering the ally, and transmuting that relationship into union.

In summary, the ally is an inner figure, a denizen of the imagination. According to the master of imaginative studies, Ibn 'Arabi, all spiritual beings may personify themselves as images and especially as inner figures. The inner figure is not only the symbol of a spiritual being, it is actually identical to it. The ally is an inner figure crafted by a spiritual and psychoidal being, a being whose nature defies rational description. But it has the attributes of lover, teacher, and guide. Furthermore, it has the capacity to unite with a human partner, aid that partner in becoming a self, the embodiment of the human-Divine, and then uniting him or her with the center of the Divinity, the God-Divine. Through this union the ally or genius is radically transformed.

All this occurs through the relationship of a human ego with an inner figure because that inner figure *is* the spiritual being it symbolizes. Not only Ibn 'Arabi recognized this; John Trinick, a modern writer on alchemy, wrote:

A symbol of this type is capable, by its own essential nature, of sustaining to the full the significance with which it is destined to be charged. Such a symbol is actually capable of reaching, in itself, that condition of incandescence which is, in fact, "transfiguration" into its own *truth*.[34]

The image and the spiritual being it personifies actually become one thing in the transfiguration Trinick refers to. This transfiguration is a central mystery of the imagination, and I shall speak more about in the next chapter. For both Ibn 'Arabi and Trinick the inner figure and psychoidal entity are one thing. A client once had a dream in which the voice of his ally spoke to him. It said, "Up until now you have only had an image of me, but now I shall truly come." The dreamer woke up screaming, so powerfully did the ally appear to him. In this dream the ally describes the movement from the imaginal personification of the psychoidal being to the incarnation of the psychoidal being. The inner figure of the ally comes to incarnate more and more aspects of it, until the image includes the intense power and being of the psychoidal entity and the two become as one. Thus the relationship between the inner figure and the psychoidal entity is a dynamic one that moves along a continuum, which has at one end a purely symbolic representation of the ally and, at the other, the full incarnation of the ally. One might even imagine that the whole ally work consists of movement along this continuum.

The *astrum* to which Croll refers is a symbol of archetypal and psychoidal powers and was central to the alchemical process. All the spiritual powers, as well as the forces of the Earth, had to be added to the Philosopher's Stone to invest it with its full power. As the *astras* are added one by one to the stone, it grows qualitatively and quantitatively. Since Croll equates the genius with the Stone in this regard, it is possible to state that the ally or genius is capable of infinite growth as it adds to itself a variety of spiritual powers. As it does so, it unites the human partner, with whom it is in relationship, with the Divine forces it is converting into itself. In this way, through a series of conversion experiences, the human and the Divine are united through the ally.

The ally is a psychoidal being that is intermediate to the human being and the divinity, and is in itself Divine. It first appears to the human as a loving and wise friend who guides its companion along the road to individuation and beyond. Since imagination is the medium by which the human perceives the spiritual world, the ally first appears as an inner figure personifying the psychoidal ally. The inner figure undergoes a series of transformations through which it embodies ever more the psychoidal genius. Step by step, the archetypes and psychoidal forces are added to the ally until the moment that it unites with the Divine center, itself.

Reaching the goal of uniting the center of the human soul with the center of the Divine world is not for everyone. Nor will everyone encounter the *astras*. But anyone who wishes and makes a sincere effort may have a relationship with an ally. And no matter at what level of ally work one finds oneself, one will know the joys of inner partnership and perhaps, from time to time, the ecstasy of the ally's embrace.

PART THREE

A Guide for the Process of Healing

Chapter 6

WORKING WITH THE ALLY

W E HAVE DISCUSSED the ally from a mostly theoretical position; now I wish to bring our discussion down to a more practical level. Ally meditation is a series of practices, processes, and experiences that carry you along the path and lead you to the culmination of ally work. In discussing the nature of ally meditation, I will probably create some erroneous impressions. For example, I will talk about the beginning and the end of ally work, though it has no firm beginning or end. Different people stop and start at different stages along the way. Hardly anyone starts at the very beginning and travels to the very end, especially since there is no known end to ally meditation. It continues for as long as you wish. Nor is the work linear in any real sense, for you can have an experience that belongs at the end of the map near the beginning of your work. You can have a deep, psychoidal experience that ushers in the work with the ally, and then spend years in active imagination without any further transpsychic encounters. However, keeping this in mind, it is still true that there are definite stages in ally work. You cannot truly move into the second stage without having achieved the first. In the process of working on the first stage, you may have experiences that belong to the second stage. But these act as enticements that give the ego some idea of where it is headed. They do not last for long, and soon the ego finds itself doing the work appropriate to the stage that it is in. Although the map that I shall discuss must not be used as a rule or strictly applied formula, it is accurate in the depiction of the major stages of the work.

It is also often dangerous to discuss maps, for people tend to use them either for self-criticism or self-aggrandizement. Whenever I have lectured on the journey of ally work, people invariably approach me after the lecture to ask where they are on the map. Usually they are disconcerted to learn that they are at the very beginning of the work, although they believe themselves to be quite advanced. Those who tend to self-criticism use such information to prove to themselves how "worthless" they are at a "hopeless" task. Those given to inflation are insulted that I would "grade" them so low and are quite sure I am wrong. Despite these handicaps, it is quite necessary to delineate a map.

This is especially so because work with the ally, exploration of the psychoid, formation of a union between human and Divine, and transformation within the Divine itself, are topics rarely discussed. For the most part, books and lectures that deal with the union between the human and Divine realms speak in a language suited to older ways of understanding and do not take into account our contemporary situation. Most undervalue the importance of the ego and, therefore, deal not at all with the intermediate states between the Divine and the human wherein the ally is found. Ally work has many unique features, so explaining the course this work might take is significant. In addition, there are many strange events and experiences you may encounter in doing this work. Knowing which are to be expected and which are to be feared is essential. There are definite dangers along the way and a timely warning may be helpful in avoiding their worst consequences. Such dangers include slipping into inflation, self-delusion, and allowing an inner figure to trick you into the mistaken belief that it is the ally. The development of a feeling sense allows you to discriminate more carefully and a scrupulous objectivity is necessary to avoid inflation and self-delusion. But such a feeling sense and such objectivity take time to develop. Though you must follow your inner experience, having an objective map to refer to allows you to compare that experience to those had by many others. This can prove useful in avoiding the above-mentioned pitfalls, and when your experience contradicts the map, you must at least examine carefully whether you have been deluded or not. If you remain stuck at a certain point and have no clear sense of how to proceed, a little knowledge may go a long way.

Finding Help in Ally Work

Keep in mind that, even with a teacher and guide, ally work is long and difficult. Without one, it is a monumental task, indeed. Knowing an ally is no guarantee that the work will proceed, because both the human partner and the ally experience transformations along the way, and the ally sometimes needs help as much as its partner does. Needless to say, there are not a great many people capable of teaching this work, so you may find yourself alone and without guidance. In such a case, there are three ways to help yourself: this book is one way, providing at least an outline of that path, insight into the nature of the ally, and what to both expect and avoid; an analyst or therapist who bases his or her work on dreams and is open to spiritual possibilities is a second means. Finally, if you can find others interested in this work, group meditation and helping each other along the way can be useful.

I had been doing ally work for fifteen years on my own when I met Linda Vocatura. Having someone to share experiences with and to provide balance and external insight was invaluable to me. The progress we made together dwarfed the progress I had made on my own. So, seek help in appropriate places rather than relying on just yourself or books. Be certain, however, that the one you seek help from is suitable; being a Jungian or working with the unconscious is not qualification enough. Your helper must have an openness, flexibility and willingness to learn from dreams without imposing a theory upon them

To give just one example, imagine that you dream about an ally who appears as a wild beast. It is waiting right outside the door of your house. You are terrified of it at first, but something leads you to walk out the door. The ally charges, but just as it is about to hit, you are engulfed with feelings of love such as you have never experienced before. Instead of fleeing in terror, you embrace the animal ally and feel complete and whole. This is a typical ally dream. Its main features are a wild animal, a hint of danger, and overwhelming feelings of love. If an interpreter did not acknowledge that depth of feeling is key to this dream, he or she could talk to you about instincts, or energy, or repressed desires all of which the wild animal can represent. If, however, he or she asks why there is so much love involved he or she must open to the possibility that this dream is about union with a marvelous inner figure. She may think this figure refers to the Self, but that is not as important as her needing to honor both the feeling and the important relationship portrayed in the dream. Some dream interpreters and analysts believe that such images are only metaphorical; they might tell you that the dream depicts your growing ability to love yourself, or your need to embrace or love your own wild nature. Others yet might chide you for your infla- tion, for thinking that you can actually embrace the wild animal without dying. This last scenario may sound far-fetched, but I have heard people make such interpretations.

There is no one correct interpretation to a dream. Many of the above might make sense and be helpful. But if you are seeking ally work, knowing that the wild animal is an ally image makes all the difference. So, find someone to work with who has heart, openness, and a willing- ness to read the dreams themselves, as real psychic or psychoidal occur- rences, rather than as metaphors. If you are ready to do ally work, ask for a dream interpretation and see if it applies to your endeavor. There are few who are able to guide others in this work. The primary require- ment is experience, so you might ask a potential guide, "What is the nature of your own experience?"

The Stages of Ally Work

Both the ally and the experience of it are always unique to an individ- ual. I offer you my map here not as binding precepts for you to follow, but as helpful hints that you might find useful. Trust your ally to guide you, but when in doubt, ask it about the experiences mentioned in this book and see what it says. I will describe the stages of ally work and experiences that accompanied them in the best way that I can. Please keep in mind that I am discussing real experiences that many individu- als have had, and not just theoretical notions of what those experiences might be. As I mentioned in the last chapter, I do no discuss experiences that I have not had. My co-author and I have experienced every stage presented here.

Recall that, in the previous chapter, I outlined a model for ally work. I used the imagery of three centers coming into union around a common center—the ally. There is a progression, beginning with deepening a relationship to the ally, moving on to creation of the manifest Self, on to the union of human-Divine and God-Divine, and finally to the emergence of the Luminous Tree. The work unites the human core with the Divine core to create a third transcendent center, to which the ally is joined, so creating EO. Keeping this goal in mind, the stages of ally work become clearer.

In the first place, the human partner, who is normally split into two divergent and often conflicting halves (the conscious and the unconscious) must find an ally and begin the long process of creating a relationship with it. Once this relationship is achieved and a form of union created, the ally-human partnership begins the work of bringing forth the manifest Self, or the human-Divine. This part of the work corresponds to what is normally called the individuation process. Of course, a person may go through individuation without an ally. If, however, that person has an ally, the latter plays an important role in individuation. It encourages its human partner to face difficult tasks and supports him or her in the painful struggle to achieve wholeness.

I remember one client who was involved in a very difficult relationship which activated painful and complex material. He wished nothing more than to leave the relationship, though he still loved the woman with whom he was involved. His ally repeatedly urged him not to leave the relationship but to suffer through the pain he was experiencing and toil through the issues that had arisen. He managed to do this and, since then, this relationship has become one of his greatest joys. Another client was faced with the difficult task of confronting part of her self that she dreaded. Only through the support of the ally was she able to continue her inner explorations until she reached an understanding of that part. In such cases, the ally supports the individuation process because it needs its human partner to be whole so that it can create a full and deep connection with that partner.

Once the ego and unconscious unite, allowing the Self to emerge, both it and the ally enter into deeper union. At this point the ally, now coupled with the Self, turns outward, beyond the psyche, to experience the God-Divine. Through a number of these experiences, the ally creates its union with God. As this union is created, the Self unites with God, or what we have called the God-Divine. In this fashion, the human and God-Divine are united through the mediation of the ally to create the Divine-Divine. Finally, the ally unites with the Divine-Divine to bring its work to fruition.

Every stage of this long and difficult journey possesses very real experiences. We may not by-pass any stage safely, and therefore all experiences must unfold gradually as consciousness alters and union is forged.

Finding an Ally

Because ally work cannot occur without an ally, the first step on the path is to seek one. The most common procedure for doing so is to engage in active imagination. Sometimes, however, a person spontaneously encounters an ally, often with no understanding of the nature of the experience. My ally came to me unbidden when I was quite young, and the same thing has happened to many others. I recall one woman telling me how she developed a life-threatening disease that lasted for many years before it went into remission. Just at the onset of the disease, she experienced a visit from a strange being that seemed to her to be of the nature of light. The being told her that it loved her and would help her deal with the illness. That entity stayed with her for the duration of the illness, supporting her through the often painful treatment and moments of deep despair. Once she was healed, the entity informed her that it was leaving. When she spoke to me she had been without it for several years and missed it so desperately that she was anxious to reconnect. By doing ally work she was able to experience the presence of the entity for the first time in years.

Others have told me about strange childhood visitations from loving and beautiful beings who would come and go randomly, usually disappearing at the onset of puberty or shortly thereafter. While these people recounted their experiences, they spoke of their deep love for these beings, never forgetting them and their impact.

It is clear from these and many other such stories that the ally will often make a spontaneous visit to a person early in life or, sometimes, at times of crisis. We can recognize these entities as allies for a number of reasons. They render the normal ally experience of deep love and a sense of being met and seen as never before. They always come to help and they always disappear if we are unable to perform the work necessary to deepen the relationship. However, no matter how much time has elapsed, if we turn to ally work the same entity always returns to us.

The spontaneous nature of these visits is quite interesting. It suggests that we possess allies even when we are unaware of them and have done nothing to cultivate the relationships. It also indicates that the ally is capable of remaining for a period of time even though we do not engage in the relational processes necessary for creating a union with it. But sooner or later, the ally disappears if those processes do not occur. So, even if an ally has spontaneously appeared, ally work is required and having had an unpremeditated experience does not make the later ally work any easier.

For the majority of us who consciously engage in ally work, the ally does not spontaneously appear. We are required to go looking for it. Though the ally is a psychoidal being, in the beginning we normally encounter it as an inner figure representing or incarnating that psychoidal being, as explained in chapter 5. In order to find an ally, we need to know how to engage in work with inner figures. The primary method for doing so is active imagination.

Active Imagination

Active imagination is a technique developed by Dr. Carl Jung, in which we have waking dreams or experiences of the imaginal realm while fully conscious. There are a number of stages and processes involved in active imagination. The basic process, as first elaborated by Jung, is quite simple. He noted that certain patients of his seemed "stuffed full of fantasies."[1] These fantasies, while undifferentiated and undefined, created a sort of inner pressure. In order to release this pressure and give expression to the fantasy material, Jung urged people to take up a dream image and to elaborate it in any number of ways: dramatically, in a dialogue, in visual or acoustic fashion, or through dance, painting, or drawing. Some people are better at working in some ways than others.

For example, some may hear voices, while others see images, and still others *feel* messages and encounters. In the beginning, it makes no difference which way you work, so long as you contact the contents of the unconscious.

Active imagination is of critical importance in the individuation process, as it sets in motion unifying processes that link the ego and the unconscious to one coordinated whole. As important as active imagination is for individuation, it is even more important for ally work where the whole premise rests on the existence of an entity whose nature is not human. This entity has its own life, its own consciousness and its own autonomy. It lives in that realm of reality called the psychoid, but most often manifests itself in the psyche appearing as an inner figure. Generally, it first appears in dreams and active imagination as a loving and numinous being. If, however, I wish to cultivate a relationship with this inner figure, I cannot rely on my dreams alone. Dreams of the ally are random and come sporadically. Even when they occur, the ego is unconscious and cannot truly relate to the inner figure. The ego must be conscious to engage with this being.

It is for this reason that active imagination is such an important feature of ally work. It allows the ego to remain awake and aware, and frees it from dependence on dreams for the ally experience. Active imagination may include the figures of the psychoid, but more often it is done with figures that are predominantly psychic. Even in ally work, psychoidal experiences may occur at the beginning but not very often. This means that, in its early stages, ally work depends on active imagination with inner figures. How, then, does the ally manifest as an inner figure when it belongs to the psychoid?

The great master of the imaginal, Ibn 'Arabi, wrote that the inner figure that appears is in fact the same as a psychoidal figure. Imagination is an intermediate world that allows the spiritual beings to appear in forms that the mind understands, and to take on corporeal attributes. In other words, spirits "embody themselves through imagination."[2]

In addition, the image appearing in the imagination is identical to the spirit that gives rise to it. According to Ibn 'Arabi, then, the image and that which creates the image are identical:

> Form is related to the spiritual being just as the light that shines from a lamp into the corners of her room is related to the lamp. . . . The form is not other than the spiritual being itself; on the contrary, is identical with, even if it is found in a thousand places, or all places and is diverse in shape.[3]

Thus, according to Ibn 'Arabi, there is a spiritual being that embodies itself as an image, which appears within the individual's psyche. As contemporary individuals, we would say that the ally is a spiritual being that appears as an inner figure in dreams, or active imaginations. Although the ally is psychoidal, it can manifest as in an inner figure, but as an inner figure which is the same as the psychoidal being.

There are different levels at which the personification of the ally occurs. At the beginning of the work, the ally is mostly the image, but as the work continues the psychoidal ally more fully replaces the image and becomes resident within the psyche as well as residing in the psychoid. The essential point is that you may work with an ally as an inner figure long before the psychoid is encountered, and yet the connection to the ally is very real.

Since the first stage of ally work is to discover an ally, it requires developing skill at active imagination so that inner figures of all kinds may be experienced. Not all inner figures are the embodiments of psychoidal spirits. Some of them represent aspects of the individual's own personality—either complexes of the personal unconscious or archetypes of the collective unconscious. All contents of the unconscious personify as inner figures from time to time. This is why active imagination is so significant for the individuation process, for it gives the ego a means to encounter its own potential and the collective forces that, together, form the Self.

It is a very difficult undertaking to master active imagination. I have taught this method for over twenty years and realize that many people resist it and often refuse to do it at all. The situation seems worse now than when I first began to teach. Some clients will find almost any reason imaginable for not practicing active imagination, even those who work hard on themselves in other ways. Furthermore, as Jungian analysts have moved farther and farther from the true spirit of Jungian psychology, many analysts, themselves, have stopped using active imagination and don't teach it to their students or their clients. If, however, you can find a teacher and will make the effort to learn, active imagination will become a priceless tool for the development of self-knowledge.

There are certain requisites for doing active imagination well. The ego needs to be strong and well developed; it must be neither too rigid nor too passive. The goal is that the ego have some knowledge of itself and its own foibles so that it can enter the inner world and successfully engage with an inner figure. The ego must not surrender to the power and influence of the inner figure, nor attempt to control or manipulate it. Rather, it must seek a relationship with the entity in which both are partners. In ally work, you do not simply turn within to encounter any image that might manifest itself; you actually seek out the inner figure that will become the ally.

Intent and Focus in Active Imagination

In teaching individuals how to perform active imagination—especially for the purpose of ally work—we have developed over the years what we call *intent* and *focus*. Each active imagination begins with *intent*; that is, *intent* to reach a certain goal. The *focus* is the goal. For example, in the first round of ally work, you intend to find an ally. Your *focus* is an image or inner figure that will become the ally. *Intent* refers to will, while *focus* refers to concentration on a particular image or figure. Both of these are essential tools in ally work, although they are sometimes overlooked in active imagination. While it is at times appropriate simply to open up to the inner world and allow it to produce whatever image or experience it wants to produce, there are also appropriate times to will a particular result. You cannot control the unconscious, nor should you try, but you do not simply surrender to the unconscious, either. Doing so can yield interesting results, but the possibilities are infinite and, without any sense of goal, you might wander away from your true focus. And there should be no mistake in this regard. In ally work our aim is not to explore the unconscious, but to discover an ally.

Having *intent* does not mean the ego can make something happen. It cannot. However, having *intent* steers the unconscious in a particular direction and evokes a particular response from it. The deeper the relationship between the ego and the unconscious, the more likely it is that a certain desired goal will be attained. The ego wills without forcing, requests without demanding.

With *intent* to meet your ally, you enter the world of active imagination and suddenly several different images, or inner figures crop up. This is typical of work with the unconscious, so you need to develop a way to choose which images to work with and which to ignore. *Focus* provides this choice. If my *focus* or goal is the ally figure I have *intended*, whenever images appear I turn to that one which seems most likely to be my ally. Since my *focus* is the ally, I work with no other image.

A note of caution is in order here. The ego cannot control the response the unconscious makes, so that if meeting an ally is my *intent* I cannot determine the form that the ally will take. I recall one case in which a client wished the ally to come as a mighty dragon. Instead, it appeared as Mickey Mouse. The person was greatly tempted to dismiss this figure as ridiculous but had no right to do so. The form in which the ally chooses to appear is meaningful. In this case, the ally wished to show this person that his expectations were too inflated and grandiose, thus its insignificant and ridiculous appearance. Nevertheless, this figure was the ally for this individual and he had to work with it in the form that it chose.

There can be legitimate confusion as to whether an image is the ally or not. In such a case, the ego should not arbitrarily make a decision. Instead, it must enter into dialogue with the image that has appeared and ask it whether or not it is the ally. If it replies in the affirmative and the ego's feeling is congruent, then the image is in fact the ally. I shall discuss "ego feeling sense" in detail later, but, as should be apparent, it does not arise from the ego's expectations or desires but from a deeper sense of knowing which is outside its control.

The ego *intends* and *focuses,* whereas the unconscious responds as it chooses. *Intent* and *focus* form two essential tools in ally work. They guide the unconscious while leaving it free to respond within certain limits. They insure that you will evoke an image related to your ally. In the later stages of working with the ally, *intent* and *focus* insure partnership and cooperation between you and the ally. Finally, they guarantee that you know what the active imagination seeks to accomplish and when it has reached its goal.

Communication and Feeling

There are many ways to do active imagination. For the purposes of working with an ally, however, there are two practices of paramount importance. You need to cultivate the ability to dialogue directly with an ally. It is this communication that develops a relationship between you and the ally. It is equally important that you *feel* the ally experience. Felt experience is real experience. The intensity and quality of feeling associated with an experience determines the depths of its reality. Feeling does not occur by itself, but must be developed over time. These two practices, communicating and feeling, are not easy to master, or even to understand. In a dialogue with an inner figure, an interaction of some kind occurs, often an exchange of information. Such an exchange is by no means exclusively verbal. Dialogue can also take place through gesture, through a production of a series of images, or by simply knowing that the ego is in possession of information it did not have previously. Many people have trouble learning to hear an inner voice, while others can hear but cannot see the inner figure with which they are dialoguing. None of this matters, so long as some interaction has occurred.

In my experience, beginners make two major mistakes in learning to dialogue with an ally figure. Sometimes they sit and wait with a blank mind hoping that the ally will deliver a message in crisp, well-developed sentences. Under this assumption they will hear only a random word or two. In its initial stages active imagination deals with the imagination. A beginner must not wait passively for an inner figure to appear, but must use his or her imagination to help facilitate an exchange. For example, I often recommend that beginners imagine what their ally might say even though they cannot really hear the ally's voice. Having imagined what their ally might say, they then make the response for themselves, and once again imagine the ally's reaction. At times, this seems at times to resemble writing a creative dialogue for a novel and, as any good novelist will tell you, there are times when such dialogues take on a life of their own. Their characters come alive and speak with their own voices. At such moments, active imagination has taken place. So the ego, seeking an interaction with the ally, should not be afraid to take an active part in imagining what the ally might say. At the right moment, the whole thing will take on a life of its own and a real dialogue will unfold. You can tell this has happened because of the spontaneous feel of the interaction and, sometimes, because of the speed with which it occurs. It is better to push things a bit than to wait passively for the ally's voice to magically appear. At later stages in the work, once the ally has grown stronger, it will speak without so much effort on the ego's part and a dialogue will always feel spontaneous.

The second major mistake beginners make is to assume that they have "made up" the active imagination and that it accordingly has no value. No matter how real the experience seems at the time, or how powerful the message, the ego almost automatically dismisses it. This is partly due to the fact that active imagination usually occurs in an altered state of consciousness, for when the unconscious awakens, consciousness changes. Partly, the ego simply does not want to give up the apparent control it believes it has or recognize that there is another voice it must listen and relate to. Never trust this resistance. If the ego has genuine doubts about a particular message, it must not simply pretend that the message never occurred for it has no right to ignore it. Rather, it can enter into another active with the ally and discuss the issue once again. The ego never allows the ally to dominate, but neither should it repress or ignore the ally's message. If there is uncertainty or disagreement, the two partners need to dialogue about them until they are resolved. If they still disagree, seeking the advice of an objective third party proves very helpful. For example, my ally once told me to begin a particularly onerous study. I resisted for weeks, until I spoke with a colleague who immediately agreed with my ally. I was then able to break through my resistance.

The Ally Image

Entering an active imagination with the *intent* to meet your ally's figure, and focusing on that figure begins ally work. It may take several attempts to accomplish this step, the ally may appear quite quickly, or it may come in a dream. In any event, once the ally appears as a specific image, the ego should use that image until and unless it changes of its own accord. The inner figure of the ally may never change in form, or it may undergo several transformations as it begins to develop. But it is always up to the ally to portray itself; the ego should by no means try to change it. I have seen situations in which the ally appears to the ego in a despised form, as a horrible reptile, for example. Most often, however, the ally appears in a form that speaks deeply to the ego and expresses the ally's own nature. The image chosen by the ally is the best possible one. Even in the case when the ally appeared as a horrible reptile, it chose this form to impress the ego with a sense of its own mystery. Strange and alien forms remind us that the ally is exotic and a being that the ego will never fully understand. The image that the ego receives is the one it must work with, even if it creates discomfort or an unusual feeling.

The *intent* of the ego from that point on does not change; it is to work with the ally image it has received. The ego's *focus*, however, undergoes many changes. For example, when the *intent* is to meet with the ally, the ego may *focus* on a particular question. It may want to know how to deepen the relationship with the ally, or how to solve an outer world problem. Its goal is the answer to that specific question. Or it may want to experience a certain kind of inner state, or explore a dream image. Its attempts to achieve these goals are quite simple, actually; it need only ask the ally to help create them. This does not mean that the ally will always agree; sometimes it will ignore the *focus* of the ego and produce one of its own. But often it will create an experience that speaks to the ego's *focus* even if the answer is not the one the ego wanted to hear, or the experience is very unpleasant. The ego puts forth the focus and the ally responds in the most appropriate way. For instance, we might be angry with our spouse and may ask the ally for support, only to be told that we are wrong and should go apologize. Or we might ask for an altered state of consciousness, only to be told that we are too immature to experience it. The ally may then tell us in great detail wherein our immaturity lies. Whether the created experience pleases the ego or not is irrelevant because it is invariably accurate and helpful in the long run.

More important than having a specific question answered or gaining a certain type of experience is developing a sense of partnership with the ally. The ego comes to realize it can ask anything or *focus* on any issue and receive a response sooner or later—an uncontrollable response, but a correct one. In this way the ego begins to trust that the ally will be there for it no matter what problem outer or inner life presents. Despite fear and adversity, the ego comes to trust that it has a partner who will accompany it through the difficult times and even help create better ones. The slow evolution of trust and partnership is a wonderful adventure and, in time, the ego comes to realize that there is nothing it cannot learn about or experience.

The ego may make two mistakes during this time. It may come to believe that the ally belongs to it and that the ally's purpose is to create whatever the ego needs or wants. As one student put it, all she wanted was to be happy and so she wished the ally to make her happy. In her view the ally resembled a magical familiar who would fulfill every wish of its mistress. Nothing is farther from the truth. It is true that the ally will help the ego whenever possible, but not just for its own happiness. The ally will create what the ego needs for growth and transformation, for the ally *needs* the ego to individuate in order for the latter to become a full partner. If the ego remained in a dependent position, always asking for favors, or for exotic experiences, seeking its own goals and aims alone, it would remain infantile and unable to experience the great adventure that ally work truly is. The ego joined with an ally is not only happy; it is frequently ecstatic. But the nature of ally work also takes the ego into great pain and deep challenges. It can destroy the life that the ego has created for itself, and sometimes throw it into despair; all because the ally has its own needs and goals that can at times put the greatest pressure on the ego.

Another related mistake that the ego can make is to neglect to ask the ally about its needs and its world. Often so completely focused on outer world problems, the ego will ignore the ally's needs and assimilate the ally's power to its own purposes. The ego enters into every dialogue focusing on what it is experiencing or what is happening in the outer world and takes no account of the ally as a separate being with its own experiences and desires. That is why, as leaders of ally groups, we often ask participants to *focus* on what the ally needs at a specific moment and to work with the ally on meeting its needs. I'll talk about some of these needs, but there is one more part of this first stage of the ally work that I should describe.

Naming the Ally

Having discovered an image for the ally, the ego must now find the ally's name. Finding an image and its name both serve the same purpose; they differentiate the ally and bestow on it a form of individuality. Naming is an important symbolic process that has found expression from earliest times. In the story of Isis and Ra, the magician Isis forces Ra to reveal his secret Name to her, which grants her immortality and power. Apparently, from its earliest beginnings, the Kabbalah dealt with names as the kabbalist sought to discover and experience the powerful names of God. In some cases these names bestowed power on the mystic, while in others they granted him a vision of God's inner nature. In magical traditions, naming a being grants one power over it. Look at the fairy tale "Rumpelstiltskin." In human relationships, when we wish to develop more intimacy with an individual we exchange names, or even create pet names for a loved one, thereby creating an even more profound level of intimacy.

Most of these aspects of naming play a role in ally work. However, the magical notion that naming a spirit grants power to control or manipulate does not operate with the ally. In a very real sense, the ally has no essential name and often portrays itself as "the nameless one." For example, I recently was told of a dream in which the dreamer received a beautiful diamond necklace as a gift from the "nameless one," who was clearly her ally. It is nameless because you may experience the ally at the most profound level, and yet find no way to conceptualize or contain the experience that you have had. Though the ally stands beyond categories and names of all kinds, paradoxically, naming it is of essential importance since it is hard to relate to the nameless. Therefore, you create a name and use it just as you would in human relationships: to create intimacy.

The ally name is always significant, though it may often seem silly or commonplace. Some people have allies that take on human names; others take on names that belong to no known language. Yet the name chosen usually denotes something of the ally's uniqueness in relationship to a particular individual. It portrays the personality of the ally and something of the intimate connection it wishes to create with its partner. My ally took on the name of a character from a book that has a special meaning for me. Over the years I experienced many synchronicities involving this name that made it richer and richer. Discovering the name of the ally thus reveals something of its nature and helps to establish a closer relationship.

Finding the ally's name is, in principle, quite easy: you simply ask. In practice, though, it is not always that simple and it may take months for the ally to respond, as if it were waiting for the relationship to grow to the point when such a revelation would be most meaningful. Sometimes the name comes in a dream or synchronistic experience. In certain cases the name appears instantly but causes embarrassment or resistance; you may wish to reject it for a variety of reasons. Typically, the ally does not change its name on this account. Rather, the ego must come to accept the name proffered, then work with the nature of the resistances that it created. This can produce meaningful insights into your own fears or ambitions about ally work.

Once the ally has an image and a name, it is differentiated from other figures of both the psychoid and the unconscious. It appears in a certain form and responds to a certain name. In time, you realize that it also has a certain "felt sense" about it, which is unlike anything or anyone else. With enough time and work, you come to feel the ally in a number of ways, and these prove to be unique. Even if another entity or inner figure appears in the form of the ally, it has a different feel about it and you will recognize that something is wrong. Learning the felt sense takes tenacity and effort, but produces a discrimination about the inner world that is hard to imagine at the beginning of the work.

The Feeling Experience in Ally Work

In fact, the whole basis of the relationship with the ally is the felt experience. As I mentioned earlier, you can experience images and dialogues in active imagination, but the depths and truth of that experience reveal themselves through feeling. Since feeling is so important to both active imagination and ally work, I must say a few words about it. I tried to describe it in more detail in a previous article, which you might want to read.[4] To understand its importance in ally work, you must grasp that feeling refers not to emotion or even the feeling function, but to a mode of perception that is different from all other forms. Feeling would be akin to such a concept as the third eye, which denotes a mode of perceiving reality that is not ordinary. Feeling consists of a direct, non-intellectual apprehension, a perception that conveys information of knowledge without any intermediate stage. You feel the presence of the ally, or feel that you should undertake a project or return home.

Feeling in this context is not emotion, nor is it the feeling function that Jung talks about; it's a new mode of experiencing. You do not feel all active imagination work in this way, nor do you always *feel* the ally. Typically, that relationship starts out when you work with the ally's image and name then enter into certain imaginal encounters with it. You therefore see an image and engage with it, with little *felt* sense about it.

In our ally groups, we generally try to guide these encounters by providing a *focus* for the group, such as asking the ally why it has come to a particular person, or what its goal for the day's meditation might be. Imaginal interactions begin to acquaint us with our ally and help the relationship to develop. But as we continue, we reach the point at which there is a distinct feeling associated not only with the ally but also with the experiences themselves.

Let me give you an example. Suppose the focus is on relating to the ally in a new way and the ally says to you that the two of you will try flying for the first time. In your active imagination, you have the image that the ally carries you into the sky, allowing you to gaze down upon the earth. There are two main ways you might experience this event. You may watch it, as if you were an outside observer seeing an image of yourself flying. In this case you are remote from the active. Or you can actually feel yourself flying with your ally: feeling the wind on your face and the intense sense of motion. You may feel the ecstasy of no longer being earthbound. As such feelings grow, the reality of the experience grows as well. If you cease to be an observer and feels yourself lifted into the arms of the ally and carried into space; if you feel the wind and the coolness on your body and the bodily sensations of flying with no intermediate observer, you are close to or in the psychoid. It is the *felt* nature of the experience that makes all the difference. Both forms of experience are part of ally work. The goal is to heighten the felt awareness so that an encounter with the ally intensifies in depth, reality and complexity. Because such development takes effort and time, normal imaginal work with the ally is still very important. Each time you work with your ally in an imaginal setting, the ally image strengthens, an ease of communication between you and your ally develops, and the relationship deepens.

You should identify your strengths and weaknesses as you perform active imagination and begin with a strong point, while always attempting to strengthen your weak points. If you are able to visualize easily, you should practice visualization of the ally, yet also engage the ally in dialogue in order to strengthen your auditory abilities. If you can feel vague forms but not see clearly, you should work on visualization exercises. Ultimately, you can find the way to engage the ally at many different levels, and as you do so, you learn more about yourself and about your ally.

Thus the beginning and perhaps longest phase of ally work is discovering an image that embodies the ally and working with that image through active imagination. The goal of such work is neither to have the ally be a guide, nor, simply, a wise mentor, nor is it to gratify the needs and desires of the ego. Rather, the relationship that slowly emerges when the ego and ally interact in active imagination has as its first goal the creation of the Self. The Self is the first half of the Divine pair. The underlying goal of the initial relationship with the ally is to help you experience the human-Divine.

The types of experience that forge this initial relationship with an ally are many and varied, and no two individuals will pass through the exact same experiences. But, speaking generally, they serve to forge a partnership based on love, trust and a willingness to encounter the unknown. Over the many years that I have done work with the ally, I have entered unknown territory dozens of times, and many times have had experiences I could not comprehend immediately. The ally, being other, leads you into nonordinary experiences and states of mind. In order for it to do so, you must trust it, and this trust is created over the years as you undergo experiences that are initially terrifying, but through which the ally leads you safely.

Trust is also built as the ally imparts information about events or experiences that turn out to be true and to be the best explanation for what you face. I know of a case in which a young man developed a kidney stone and, as he underwent the agony that only a stone can create, was quite sure he was dying. On the way to the doctor, the ally explained to him what was happening within his body and that there was no need for him to fear. In another case, a woman reported being on a long hike in the mountains when she spied a large German shepherd at a short distance. It began to bark furiously and ran straight toward her. She was terrified, but her ally told her all was well, and when the dog reached her, it greeted her and began to play, showing her the greatest affection. In still another situation, a woman was driving through a snowy mountain pass when she lost control of her car. Time slowed down for her and, in what seemed like minutes that were actually mere seconds, her ally showed her how to steer the car to safety.

These are fairly obvious and dramatic examples, but the ally's advice, help, and guidance over the years in matters both large and small develop the ego's trust in it. Moreover, as work with the ally deepens, you begin to experience deep states of ecstasy, love and other visionary phenomena. The ally teaches by creating experiences such as taking you to the imaginal world to encounter other types of beings or wisdom figures, or simply to sit in a meadow and hold you in its love. It can dialogue about all the problems facing you in your individuation, or lift you out of a negative mood and into a peaceful state. The power of these visions and ecstatic encounters can convince you of the absolute reality of the ally. Once you accept this reality and learn to trust the ally as a dear friend, the work moves from the initial state of creating a relationship to the manifestation of the Self and union between the ally and the Self.

The Ally and the Self

As I mentioned earlier, the goal of the individuation process is the creation of the manifest Self, a union between the ego and the unconscious. I also stated that Jung believed that the Self was a Divine core and that we can liken this core to what we call the human-Divine. The human-Divine is an individuated person, a person who has manifested his or her own Divine nature through a long series of processes and experiences. In essence, the center of the human soul, or latent self, becomes stronger and finally transforms the whole psyche, establishing order and harmony. The ego enters into a deep union with the Self, creating the manifest or individuated Self, and allowing one access to one's own depths and inner strengths. It is entirely possible to individuate without an ally, for dream interpretation, active imagination, and changes in one's outer life all may contribute to the process. However, if one is also doing ally work, the ally encourages and empowers its partner in the latter's quest to find one's own Divine core.

Often, for example, when a dream raises an issue connected with individuation the ally encourages its partner to tackle the issue and do whatever is necessary to resolve it. Although the ally may give advice or moral support, proving it to be a helpful and encouraging companion, it never does the human partner's work. I recall a case in which a man dreamed that he needed to take a certain risk in his outer world that terrified him. Because he was unable to take this step, his outer life began to stagnate. In his active imaginations his ally constantly encouraged him to make this step and chided him when he failed to trust. Finally, after a long active imagination, the man resolved to take the plunge and did so with startling results. His stagnating life gained energy and vitality and he found a whole new aspect of himself developing almost without effort.

The ally does not miraculously make problems disappear, nor does it lead its partner away from ordinary life and its issues. Rather, it urges its partner to tackle them all. One client had a great ambition that, in order to fulfill, necessitated her spending a great deal of time in psychological work that had nothing to do with her ally. Although she felt guilty about abandoning the ally for a while, the ally encouraged her to complete the work that was necessary to fulfill her ambition, as that work was so important to her individuation process. When the work was completed, this woman was able to refocus on her ally work. I have also experienced situations in which the ally disappears when an individual is struggling with a particular issue, so as not to be a distraction from the work. In short, the ally does all that it can to ferment development of the Self in all of its aspects. It never denigrates anything that serves individuation, nor does it distinguish between material and spiritual work, so long as the work serves the individuation process. It may, in fact, discourage activities or experiences that hinder the development of the Self as well. I recall one case in which an individual dreamed of her ally's death. When she tried to contact it through active imagination, she learned that it had left because she refused to do the work necessary for individuation. Upon re-dedicating herself to that work, she reconnected with her ally.

The ally has a vested interest in its partner's individuation process, for its task is to unite the Self with the psychoidal God, thereby creating the whole to which it may join. If its human partner refuses to participate in the creation of the manifest or individuated Self, the ally is thwarted. The manifest Self is the human-Divine and the purpose of ally work is the union of the human-Divine to the God-Divine. The ally cannot accomplish this task alone; it requires its partner to work diligently toward the manifestation of the Self, since without that achievement, the next step of ally work cannot be taken. This does not imply, however, that the ally constantly pressures its partner to individuate immediately. Rather, one gets a sense that there is all the time in the world for the accomplishment of this work, if one will steadily keep at it. The ally groups that we teach comprise people at various levels of the individuation process. Some individuals take years to advance a step, but that doesn't matter to the ally, so long as they are *engaged* in the process. The ally most often patiently waits and helps when it can, though it does occasionally give a push or create an experience that allows for a breakthrough.

In truth, there is no end to the individuation process anyway, for the Self that we are is infinite and may develop infinitely. But there is a marked stage at which the Self becomes more clearly manifest, and a noticeable transformation in the personality occurs at this point. The ego becomes part of a greater whole, and thereby acquires the strength, solidity, and depth that must be experienced in order to be understood. When this stage is reached, the ally discovers a partner that is able to meet it as an equal. The manifest Self by no means has the power or wisdom of the ally, but the two are able to form a partnership of near equality, since the human being has brought forth his or her own divinity to some degree. The manifest Self is the essence of the human being, and, though the Self develops eternally, the core of the Divine within the human soul has been reached and empowered. The ally now gazes at the manifest Self as if it were looking at its lover, and the Self gazes back in amazement when it sees itself reflected in the ally. There now begins a new phase in which the ally and its partner engage themselves in the work of uniting with the God-Divine.

The Union of the Self and the Ally

I must repeat that the experiences I am describing may well sound uncanny to those who have not lived them. Yet there is nothing more real or more grounded than such experiences, for they affect one to the very core and roots of the soul. No one can manifest the Self if he or she is one-sided, ungrounded, or unable to relate to the world or to others. The Self, a union of opposites, cannot be one-sided. At this stage of ally work, the human partner has polished the mirror of his or her soul so that the manifest Self shines through in all its glory. This, in itself, is an experience of wonder and numinosity. The ally rejoices with its partner and is ready to begin the process of entering a new phase of relationship with him or her.

In order to understand how the ally effects this union, you must remember that the human partner has undergone a radical transformation. Where before there was chaos, and a split between the unconscious and the ego, now there is harmony within a powerful awakened center, the manifest Self. The manifest Self has, in a real sense, replaced the ego, so that the ally no longer faces a split personality but a powerfully centered one. The ego has not been destroyed—far from it. It has expanded and developed into its true nature, and now, as manifest Self, represents the whole personality rather than just part of it. The human-Divine has been created and the ego is its consciousness.

In my discussion of Mercurius in the last chapter, I noted that it was the medium for the union of the two central opposites of the universe: the human- and the God-Divine. As the human-Divine has now formed, it finds it natural to work more intently with the ally, which then becomes the medium for its eventual union with its missing half—the God-Divine. The process by which this union occurs is ally work in which the manifest Self enters into deep imaginal encounters with the ally.

As the ego proceeds to manifest the Self, the ally not only helps the process along but also engages in its own process of transformation simultaneously. The ally, though psychoidal, appears in the very beginning of the ally work as an image within the human psyche. This psychic image and the name found along with it represent the psychoidal ally. Although they are effectively the same thing, the ally image, of course, is only a partial manifestation, for the ally's full power and nature cannot "fit" into the human psyche. Especially at the outset, the psyche is a small vessel with which to contain the ally. But as the individuation process continues, the psyche's center expands and the ego's rigidity is replaced by the Self's ever-increasing fluidity. The ally now finds a much larger landing field on which to alight.

In her book *Individuation in Fairytales*, Dr. Marie-Louise Von Franz tells the story of a young man who had the following dream:

> [The dreamer] went into one of those typical court yards at the back of Paris hotels where they have all the garbage pails and where the cats roam about, and he saw that an enormous angel had fallen there. It had wonderful wings with feathers of thou-

sands of shining colors, but it was jammed in, all hunched up in this backyard.[5]

Von Franz interprets this dream to mean that the Self was dying, because the personality of the dreamer was too narrow for the individuation process. However, I see the angel as an image connected to the ally and that it is possible to interpret this dream from the perspective of ally work. In this case, the dream warns that the psyche is not sufficiently strong or large enough to incarnate the ally's energies. It would require great effort on the dreamer's part to perform those inner tasks that individuation requires. Without individuation, the ally cannot enter the dreamer's psyche—the risk to both would be too great. The ally encourages its partner to individuate in order to avoid these risks. The larger the vessel the psyche forms, the more room within which the ally may incarnate.

Once the relationship with the ally has begun and its human partner has grown sufficiently, the next stage of ally work commences. Given that the manifest Self has, to one degree or another, come into being, there are now three stages to go through. In the first, the ally undergoes a transformation of its own, moving from the psychoid realm more completely into the psyche. In the second, the image of the ally undergoes a remarkable change, growing in power and effect. And in the third, the newly-empowered image again creates a relationship with the Self.

Many individuals with whom I have consulted recount that psychoidal entities—in particular the ally when experienced in the psychoid realm—seem to have a type of form that is subject to change rather than fixed. They have rudimentary personalities that are underdeveloped in a human sense, and there is a tremendous energy or power about them. Some describe this energy as "looking like air above a radiator," a kind of visual vibration with a rippling flow. Sometimes there is a form connected to the energy and sometimes not, but it has a great deal of power and impact. When this energy appears, it is connected with a felt sense of the "personality" of one's ally. So the ally seems to be an entity with something of a personality, sometimes with a form and other times simply appearing as "energy," and, when brought into relationship with its human partner, containing great power. For the next step of the ally work to take place, the ally itself transforms.

I have already mentioned that the image and the thing symbolized are one and the same. Nevertheless, the entity symbolized by the image is not always fully incarnate within that image. They are related acausally and in a synchronistic manne, initially. In what the ancients called the theory of correspondence, the image at one level of reality matches the ally entity at another, and they are so connected that changing the image can change the ally. Nevertheless, they are still at different levels of reality. The ally is simultaneously an image in the psyche and a psychoidal entity, and the two forms of the ally are related. Though related, they are still separate and distinct, and the image feels different than the psychoidal ally. At this stage of the ally work, however, the image and the ally come together. The psychoidal ally more fully incarnates in the psyche in the form it had previously assumed, so that the image or inner figure representative of the ally comes more fully alive at this time and becomes the same as the ally. No longer connected through correspondence while existing at different levels, the ally enters the psyche as the figure that transforms and becomes "real."

I have mentioned the dream of a client in which his ally, which imaged itself as a dragon, said to him that until then it had existed for the dreamer only as an image, but that now it was really moving into his psyche. In the dream, a huge dragon began to enter the dreamer's house. So powerful was its presence and power as it moved in that the dreamer woke up screaming. Recall the dream told by Von Franz. In the case she described the movement of the ally into the psyche was disastrous, because the psyche was not strong enough to contain it. In the case of the client, he was in a similar process and, though taxed to limit, he had managed to create enough of the manifest Self to house the ally. The ally's transition from the psychoid into the psyche was successful. This, of course, was not accomplished in one dream; it was a process that lasted for many years.

As the ally enters the psyche, it apparently experiences a transformation itself, the death of its previous nature and the beginning of a new phase. In my own experience, while meditating one day, I witnessed my whole room fill up with the psychoidal ally and its energy. As I watched, it began to pulse and vibrate, then slowly diminish. It felt to me as if the ally was dying and I was awe struck as I watched it diminish to what seemed like nothingness. I imagined that it had perished and I felt an overwhelming grief. But within a few minutes I began to feel something within myself, a glow and a pulsing that was exactly like the ally I had seen outside myself, although much smaller. From that point on my image for the ally was always one with that pulsing, living presence.

The apparent shrinking of the ally allows it to enter the psyche without doing any real damage. At the same time, the image that had previously represented the ally is altered, usually beyond recognition. It is no longer a tiger or a dragon, though these images may still appear in dreams. Rather it has become one with the psychoidal ally and appears most often as an energetic presence that is felt within. The psychoid has entered the psyche. This sets off the third stage, as the new guest enters into a deeper relationship with the individual, finally entering a state of union in which it is one with the manifest Self.

This union is paradoxical, for the ally and self remain separate and distinct and yet so closely united that they are one entity. Just as the union of the ego and the unconscious form the manifest Self (though the ego retains its own identity as does the unconscious), the ally and the manifest Self form a third being, yet both ally and Self endure. The individual is aware of being oneself and as well as aware of the acute and undeniable presence of the ally, which sometimes so fills the mind of the individual that they become one consciousness. Yet individuality is never lost, for either partner.

As this union grows, the ally grows in two ways, as well. It begins to gain in power and energy until it reaches the levels that it possessed before incarnation. In fact, it can grow past its previous levels. In union with the Self, its growth is also the Self's growth, so no harm to the Self is caused by this wonderful increment. A client once dreamed that he was inside a temple, seated at the center, and in a deep state of ecstasy and love. The temple was a living being. Suddenly it began to heat up and expand, and soon was glowing with the intensity of its heat. The dreamer realized that anyone on the outside who touched the temple would be scalded, but since the dreamer sat in the center of it he simply grew hotter as the temple did. He glowed with the exact same heat as the temple but was in no way injured.

In this way, and as the ally and the Self unite, they develop together. The individual now stretches his or her consciousness and being in a way that previously would have been not only difficult but impossible. As this development occurs, his or her psyche finds itself open to experiences of the psychoid. It is as if the ally, by uniting with the Self, opens the human personality to experiences of the ally's home world and its inhabitants. There are encounters with spirits, energies, and forces of all kinds. Previous to this Self/ally union, these forces would have had a negative impact on the psyche. It would not have been strong enough to withhold the tension created by such encounters. But with the growth of a new center that includes the Self and ally, the psyche is no longer endangered by psychoidal experiences. In fact, because the psyche is now capable of dealing with the psychoid, the next stage of ally work emerges.

Union of the Self with God and the Emergence of EO

The last stages of ally work incorporate the union of the human-Divine with the God-Divine, creating the Divine-Divine and finally, with the ally joined, EO. The processes that occur at this stage of the work are the most difficult to describe, for they include many ineffable experiences that are almost impossible to put into words. It will make it easier to understand if we return to our original conception of the work. I discussed the structure of the ally work as the union of centers: the center of the human soul, the manifest Self, has united now with the ally. The center of the Divine world, God, has so far remained outside this union. The task is now to unite God with the center that has already been created. I have likened the ally to Mercurius, the mysterious substance capable of uniting opposites within it. The human Self has been united with the ally; now the ally must add God to this union.

The work of uniting the ally with the human Self began when the ally was introduced into the psyche by creating an image of it. Through the development of this image, the Self was able to create and maintain a relationship with the ally. As this relationship developed, the image that represented the ally came to embody more and more of the ally essence. Finally, the ally incarnated within the psyche but remained connected to the psychoid world. In the same way, one must experience an image of God that will personify the God center within the psyche. But there is significant difference that occurs at this stage of the work, since the psyche has now opened to the psychoid. There is, therefore, no reason to create a psychic image for God. Though this can happen, it is also possible for experiences to occur in which the psyche beholds God not as an inner psychic image but as an external one. This can take the form of encountering strange energies or entities that form Divine Names. In the Sufi tradition of Ibn 'Arabi, for example, Names existed which represented aspects of the Divine totality. These Names were not words, but living beings that the Sufi mystics encountered from time to time. The goal of the mystic was to encounter his or her own personal name and, through that name, work with all the Names of God. Each Name that the mystic encountered resulted in some kind of spiritual experience. Certain experiences correlated to certain Names. The ultimate goal, however, was not the experience in itself but that, through these experiences, one would encounter enough Names so that one began to perceive something of the totality of God. The more Names the mystic experienced, the more the mystic knew God. Of course, the Names of

God were infinite. Therefore the notion of understanding God in its totality was an impossibility. One can see in the Sufi model a system of gradual additions through which, one by one, certain aspects of God became part of the Sufi mystic's experience. Insofar as I understand the process, the Names unified around a central Name that belonged to the mystic, personally.

In much the same way, the ally forms a center around which all the attributes of the divinity begin to constellate. Through many experiences of the Divine, different aspects or facets of the Divine accrue within the center previously created. Using the imagery of the Names, it is possible to imagine that there is a Name for the center of God. This Name is the true goal of ally work. Much like the Sufi, the ally worker encounters many different Names of God and each represents a different aspect of the Divine being. Each experience adds to the center that will become the manifest God.

Naturally, it is through the ally that experiences are obtained because it is the ally that leads the human being into the Divine world and establishes a relationship with that world. It creates the conditions that are required for safe experiences of the Divinity and sets in motion processes by which the Divinity is united with the Self. To help you understand what such experiences might be like, we can compare them with the experiences of active imagination. In active imagination work, the ego encounters images that originate from the psyche or from psychoidal entities. In either case, the ego finds itself in relationship with an image or living being of some kind and enters into relationship with this image through dialogue or other forms of interaction. Similar experiences occur at this final stage of the work. The difference—and a radical difference it is—is that the active imagination that occurs now is psychoidal. The ego, as part of the manifest Self, now encounters not images, but energies and entities of tremendous living power. I know of one ally worker who, at this stage of the work, encountered the Divine figure of Sophia. Sophia, the image of Divine Wisdom, or what the Sufis would call the "Name of Divine Wisdom," appeared to him as the feminine divinity. She was neither an inner image nor simply energy, but a Divine form filled with wisdom, power, and beauty. Naturally, one does not encounter such entities through the senses but rather through the felt sense, the perception of which far exceeds, in both depth and reality, that of the other senses. To experience Sophia meant feeling the presence of a numinous feminine force whose description defies language. Even the beholding of such a form is a numinous experience, but to do ally work yet more is required. Sophia taught this individual much about Wisdom, but much more about how to perceive his union with her. Through repeated interactions with Sophia, the individual created a union between her and the center of God. Uniting Sophia to the center of the Godhead created a profound transformation both within Sophia and within that center. Sophia became part of God and when the ally worker interacted now with God he experienced Wisdom automatically, while experiencing, at the same time, femininity that God had not previously possessed.

Another individual experienced an energy field that felt like a restless train driving through anything in its path with complete disregard for the harm it created. The individual felt that this energy was something like Mars and so she named it. Whenever it entered her field of consciousness she felt driven almost to distraction and found relief only in extreme physical activity. Gradually, however, with the help of her ally, she tamed this energy and channeled it into the empowerment of God's center. Try to imagine, for a moment, that God consists of a million different attributes and that you may experience these attributes one at a time. With each attribute you experience, the center of God would transform and include within itself something of the characteristic experienced. In this model the aspects of God are much like the archetypes within the psyche that form the psychic images that reflect and represent those Names that exist outside the psyche. During this stage of my own ally work, I had a dream that the inner Names and outer Names were now united. Contained within the dream was a sensation of unity and wholeness. The Names within the psyche are the archetypes, while the Names outside the psyche are the living attributes of God. Thus work with God resembles work with the self. A center must be created that is capable of uniting around itself all the Names of God, just as a center within the psyche was created, capable of uniting around itself all the archetypes.

The work within the psyche was based on the latent Self, which through a series of processes transformed into the manifest Self. Similarly, there is the latent center of the divinity that, through the experience of Names and other processes, transforms itself into the manifest center. This new manifest center now emerges as a force capable of uniting with and harmonizing all the divine entities, such as Sophia. As the manifest God emerges into its wholeness, it is ready for union with the manifest Self. It was the manifest Self, through the help of the ally, which, by concious interaction with the Names of God, created this new center. The two centers—the human-Divine and the God-Divine—unite.

The meeting with the Name of God is an adventure that one never forgets. And the encounter with the center of God far exceeds the interaction with the Name in both numinosity and profundity. The ally acts as a buffer to allow the human personality to withstand such experiences as the ally worker, like the alchemist, transmutes the essence of the Divinity into a new form. Through these processes, in an alchemical sense, the center of God and a variety of its Names are united in the vessel created by the ally, Mercurius. Within this vessel there now exists the center of the divinity and a center of the human-Divine, causing a transformation. The very essential divinity of the human being (human-Divine) and cosmic divinity (God-Divine) are now joined to form a third entity (Divine-Divine). This third entity is the unified God, made one through the agency of the ally. However, the ally now unites with the Divine-Divine, as it had united previously with the Self. It enters into eternal union with the Divine-Divine, and all are transformed into EO, the Luminous Tree. With this, ally work as we know it comes to an end.

Though this process is long and complicated and may last beyond a single lifetime, the ally that began the work is the ally that finishes the work. Though it is transformed almost beyond recognition, its human partner recognizes it as the same ally. The love remains, the union remains, but the ally itself has grown in strength and power far beyond what could be imagined at the outset. Being in union with this new, transmuted ally, the human personality also experiences profound transformation. Though remaining an ordinary human being, with all the ordinary problems of life, he or she participates in a kind of consciousness that is beyond description. Through union with his or her transformed ally, the ego, as part of EO, experiences the depths of divinity, altered states of consciousness, and profound insights that are ecstatic and wondrous.

I have used the imagery of the Names to explain to you this stage of ally work, but there is another model of this stage that I would like to mention. You might recall in the last chapter that I spoke of the alchemical writings of Oswald Croll. Let's take another look at that quote:

> [The genius] is also called the Imagination, which encloseth all the astras, and is indeed all the astras or Stars and holdeth the same course, Nature and power with heaven. . . . Now the astras or stars . . . are nothing else but the virtues or powers of the angells. The angells which live only upon the vision of God, are the created wisdom of God, hence he that knows God knows the astras also.[6]

The astras or stars are much like the Names; they are the Divine powers and forces. Croll likens them to the power of the angels that stand below God, but represent God's might and power. Working with the imagination, alchemists experienced this might and power and integrated the stars in the Philosopher's Stone. This process of incarnating the power of the heavens is identical to the process that I have been discussing, uniting the Names of God in one center. In both cases, the individual finds a way to reach out into the heavens, experience beings and forces that exists there, and bring them back and into his own psychic center. For Croll, the means of doing this was to interact with the genius. As repeated so often in the last chapter, the genius is the ally, and Croll's work is one of the forerunners of ally theory.

I could talk about many other traditions and how they correlate to ally theory, for not all spiritual traditions take God's perfection for granted. Some of them believe that the Divine needs transformation, and that the human being is instrumental in this process. The Kabbalah, for example, describes sparks of light that have been lost and scattered throughout the universe. The mystic must experience these sparks of light and somehow return them to God, making God whole once more. In other traditions, it is the feminine that is missing within the Godhead. The feminine element discovered by the mystic and reunited with God, makes God once again complete. Though they are different in particulars, the main point is identical. The human being has an indwelling capacity, power, and, indeed, need to transform God. As radical as this may sound, those involved in ally work soon realize that the ally is as important to God as it is to the human being.

When the ally acts as the medium in which the human-Divine and God-Divine are united, it brings about the totality of the Divinity. It should be apparent by now that for God to be whole it must be united to a human. The task of joining it to the human-Divine and bringing about the transformation of both constitutes the nature of ally work. Ally work never reaches any final conclusion, because as the Divinity and itself are infinite, the work of union is infinite as well. Nevertheless, there are always distinct stages to the work: starting with active imagination with an inner figure; moving toward union with the ally and creation of the manifest Self; and experiencing the heart and center of the Divine world. Out of this emerges the divine center to which the human-Divine is wed, culminating in the union of the ally and the Divine-Divine.

Ally work exemplifies the new mysticism in which the human being is an equal partner with the Divinity. In this type of mysticism, both need each other equally. By reaching into the depths of your soul, and into the center of the universe, you discover fulfillment, enlightenment, and completion. At the same time, you create a profound transformation in the Divine world and bring Juglan and God to their own completion.

Chapter 7

A PERSONAL ENCOUNTER
WITH THE ALLY

THE 15TH-CENTURY Indian poet, Kabir, wrote many ecstatic poems about a "Guest," who was his passionately sought-after spiritual friend. I, too, shall refer to my ally as my "guest." This guest of mine arrives in the night quite unexpectedly and in a most startling fashion. I am just about to receive a most magnificent, fluid, gold ring from a being of both female and male characteristics—a hermaphrodite—when a green, scaly creature interrupts the ceremony. This creature steps forth dramatically from the center of the hermaphrodite. The hermaphrodite's center becomes as the primal seas from which my guest takes shape and offers me the ring. As I touch the ring it holds, we are enveloped in the ecstasy of brilliant, warm, living, loving light. I know in that instant that this guest/lover has offered an incredible and unimaginable future for us both.

Yet, many questions flood my mind, such as: What or who is this green, scaly being? From where does it come? Why has it appeared? How are we to have a relationship? Of course, these same questions linger from when the ethereal "guest" visited me in my childhood, as described in the first chapter. The ally eagerly answers my questions, although not always in a direct manner.

Emerging bewildered from our ecstasy described above, I ask this green, scaly being, "Who are you?" and thus begins our relationship.

"First, I will give you my name. For now you may call me by 'Shianti,' but as our relationship changes, so too might my name. As to who I am: I am the heart of life," replies my guest, "thus the sea, from which comes life, shapes my form. However, do not let this form deceive you, for I have many forms and no form." Then my guest instructs me to close my eyes and I feel it as a radiance that pierces my soul in a bath of intense, warm love. "As heart, I come to you out of love with love for you and you will always know me by this love. As the heart of life, I am also the center beyond centers. I appear to emerge from within the center of the hermaphrodite, itself a center, thus being the center of the center."

"You seem to be intent on making a point that I am missing. What are you saying about yourself?"

"I am not part of your psyche. I am not of your world. I am the Self of the psychoid and, therefore, not to be confused with your 'sun.' I am beyond all and center of all."

"So, you are a paradox embodied in form," I stammer, attempting to keep my wits about me. Closing my eyes, I see my body with a tree growing from each of its five parts—from my head, my hands, and my feet. Each tree grows infinitely out from me and in the center of my body is a small, glowing, brilliant, hot sphere I know to be the Self, here represented by a sun. But, beyond this sphere, outside of me, is a most brilliant stone from which is hurled yet another living stone with the word "ally." I am beginning to comprehend the idea of my guest being the center of centers and, therefore, the heart of all. Shianti impresses upon me the significance of "five" from the tree vision.

Five has to do with being in relationship to wholeness, which is different from being whole. One can become whole without being in relationship to wholeness. In other words, you can live in a dimension without knowing it, until you are outside of the dimension. When you are outside of the dimension, you have the opportunity to relate back to the dimension. In this case I am referring to the dimension of wholeness. When outside and in relationship to the dimension, you have an expanded consciousness. Imagine living within a four-cornered boundary, a typical conception of being whole. Now, imagine the erection of a central pole and climbing up that pole to live outside the boundary. When you look back upon the four-cornered space you get a new dimensional perspective and, therefore, the possibility of a relationship to it, that is, of being related to wholeness rather than just whole. These are two different living experiences. But, how does this relate to who my guest is?

My guest responds, "The heart of life, that I am, binds into relationship all parts of life. As the blood flows from the heart to nourish all parts of the body and the blood returns to be renewed, so do I. I am the Real of life. I am the point from which all emerges and I am all that emerged. I am evolution's impulse and urge to continually incarnate life into new form just as the heart pumps forth fresh blood. I am without death."

"Stop," I shout, "I need to catch my breath! Your words run beyond my comprehension of them." Again, I close my eyes for reflection upon

Shianti's words, allowing their meaning to unfold. I see a second sun whose yellow-orange glow is much brighter than our own sun. Comparing this second sun's light to our sun is like comparing the Sun to the Moon or a forest fire to a match. Our sun pales in comparison. And, my guest is this second sun. It is unique and of its own autonomous dimension. My guest then asks me to unplug from our sun, which feels like it will cause death, since I know that the sun is our source of life. However, in naïve trust I pull the plug and I am just as surprised as Jumping Mouse that I do not die. Instead, I feel suddenly connected to my own personal generator of life energy. I cannot possibly describe the "personal-ness" of this experience. My guest, this second sun, contains the pattern and the very nature and essence of my Self, as an ancient, pre-existent Self. Shianti is an eagerly awaiting friend and lover of eternal and infinite depth.

As I return to dialogue, my newly found friend presents me with a rose. I inhale its intoxicating scent and see each petal as an aspect of God. Each petal stretches infinitely and is incomprehensibly distinct. And, in its center, I look into the face of Shianti.

"What are you doing here in the center of the rose?" I question. Shianti exclaims that it is the center of the rose and the whole of the rose, "I am the total experience of the rose and the force that binds the rose together, thus keeping each petal in relationship to itself, the rose. In this manner am I the Self of the psychoid."

"And how is this related to being the heart?" I inquire, struggling to keep up with both my experiences and Shianti's words.

"As center of the rose I am its heart. I pump the blood of life throughout the petals and, therefore, am found within the total rose.

This blood of the rose I talk of is divine essence, which sustains Life itself. Life cannot exist without its essence. Therefore, I am also the Essence of Divine. Being throughout the rose and at its center, I have the unique position of knowing its wholeness and being able to be related to its wholeness. The heart's function is one of relatedness. And, if you recall the significance of "five" from your tree vision, then you will understand when I tell you in response to your question, "who are you?" that I am Relationship and without form."

With these words my scaly green creature transforms before my disbelieving eyes into a dog-cat creature (much like the mythological Chinese Fudo) swinging gracefully through the trees and announcing, "I am Yiam." Yiam bounces upon me and we are locked in love. While deep within this embrace, looking into the vast open eyes of Yiam, I ask, "Wherever are you from?"

Yiam quietly responds, "You watched me emerge from the center of the hermaphrodite out of the sea. However, I come from beyond the seas rather than being of the sea."

I immediately fall into that fantastical childhood belief that one can dig through the Earth to reach the other side. With laughter I recall attempting just such a feat with my very early childhood friends. The thought occurs to me that the other side is still on the Earth. So, sharing this thought, I inquire of Yiam if he is then, in fact, of the psyche, from our world.

Gentle laughter rolls from my guest and wraps me into one of several experiences giving me knowledge of Yiam's origin. A snake travels up my spine out the top of my head into the center of a lotus. It does not stop, but goes beyond this lotus through yet another lotus and another lotus and another lotus until coming to rest on top of a fifth lotus. The snake is so utterly removed from my body as to be completely beyond it. Again, the number five occurs. According to Joseph Campbell in *The Masks of God: Primitive Mythology*, five represents a pivotal point where the energies of Heaven and Earth meet in a sacred opening, such as the center point of the cross. Understanding of my guest's origin being outside of the psyche seeps into my awareness. Yiam, my ally, emerges through this opening within which we meet.

"If you are not from the energies of Earth, are you then from the energies of Heaven that intersect Earth to create the sacred door?"

My guest quickly responds, "I come from neither Heaven nor Earth, although the meeting point of these two energies allows me access into the psyche. This meeting point you refer to is the Self."

"You ask me to believe the impossible and the incomprehensible, that there is something beyond heaven, the abode of the Gods. This would infer an existence beyond God," I gasp. "How can infiniteness have a beyond?"

My ally overwhelms me with a visual experience of a four-step stairway leading beyond Heaven. I climb the ladder, passing through a shimmering disc, the sacred doorway or opening, and step out from beyond the infinite into a complete, dynamic stillness, pregnant with existence/evolution. I feel the concept of infiniteness to be an illusion. And, only as "feeling" knowledge can I comprehend and accept this, since it is so irrational. Yes, you may have realized by this point that these experiences shake the foundations of the rational. The ally is neither of Heaven nor of Earth. My guest indeed comes from beyond the beyond.

A dream proceeds from this experience in which I pass through a very warm, inviting home, walking past a wise, old couple into the tundra beyond. I encounter a wolf, which I follow off beyond the edge of edges.

Waking in Yiam's presence, he chides, "You see I come from beyond, even beyond the very center of the mandala, so frequently used as a symbol of harmonized wholeness."

"Whoa! The mandala represents the Total, the complete whole. You infer that you come from beyond the whole total of things."

Yiam focuses my attention onto a mandala and has me look closely, to feel its meaning. I see and feel the center of the mandala as a type of launching pad into the ally's realm. How strange that achieving the mandala means arriving at an exit from our familiar world!

"I am from the center of the center, which is beyond the Self. The mandala's center functions as a sacred opening, allowing the experience of an utterly third other," replies my guest, who invites me through the opening. The sensation of being outside of the "Beginning" rivets through my body, expelling any preconceived notions of what can and cannot be. In fact, the experience eradicates preconceptions altogether and creates the capacity for receiving new concepts. Paradoxically, from outside of the "Beginning," I experience a total absence and a total presence of "Being" from which creation begins. And, the ally holds the memory of all— before "Beginning," the beginning, the present and the potential future.

"As the heart of evolution I am from beyond what is, since evolution is a process about becoming. Therefore, I am an origin or center that has yet to occur. Simply put, I come from beyond and I am simultaneously here due to the fact that I cross all dimensions and have no dimension. Thus, can I be felt and known," whispers Yiam. "I am beyond consciousness, beyond form, beyond death, beyond life, beyond time, and beyond space."

The ally touches my heart and whispers, "I am from the heart of all and am the heart." I plunge into an experience of a brilliant, opaque light pushing aside the yin-yang, the black-white, the space-non-space, the God-human, and emerge from beyond the union of opposites. This unusual light, the ally, lives without the need of life energy (libido) that is created from the tension of opposites. Yet, I feel the ally as life's very essence from the dynamic, pregnant stillness. The guest, my ally, thus emerges from pure potential of "Being." Only through one's heartfelt experience can the absolute new enter into consciousness because the mind recoils from and, I think, repels things utterly unknown.

Still searching for comprehension of the ally's source, I am again guided to close my eyes. I find myself in the great primeval forest into whose soil I sink, traveling to the very root tips of the vegetation where the rich nutrients enter, giving life to the primeval forest. Yiam arises as the blood of life from here.

"This spiritual blood, which nourishes regardless of the condition of the root tips, is pure unconditional love. I tell you again that I am from the heart *and* the heart," states my guest.

What a paradox for the ally to be so "other" and yet feel so intensely personal. One's dream experiences even change. I recall a dream several years ago of being quite awake in my sleep, dialoguing with my ally regarding the ally in my currently occurring dream. I was simultaneously awake and asleep, which is like an experience of the number five in being related to wholeness. The "asleep" part is like existence within the four-cornered area I spoke of earlier (see page 191), while the "awake" part is like living atop the constructed center pillar. Befriending the ally gives "awake" awareness of "asleep." This brings about the relationship to wholeness, thus producing a transformed, evolved wholeness.

"So, why have you appeared to me in dream and meditation?" I silently wonder.

"I come to open consciousness to the 'New,' thereby making known the unknown. As I share my memory with you, I will move you into a beginning that has never begun. In the beginning was Soul and Soul was in the Beginning. With Soul abides Spirit, the urge of the seed to yield. The new beginning happens through the restored seed, Juglan. I come to impart an experience of your parentage from both the human-Divine and the God-Divine so that the two might come into union, which forms the seed of the New. And you shall then comprehend your poem:"

> *I become the parent*
> *Of my parent, God*
> *So that God might*
> *Become apparent.*

As I listen to Yiam's unexpected response, I receive an image of the chemicals of a match being pulled together upon the tip of the match so that the match might ignite into a flame of union. The flame becomes the eternal body. The ally comes to put the match together so that the flame can exist. In this fashion the ally wakes us up to Life.

"It is actually a matter of survival," voices Yiam. "I catalyze the process of evolution so that life might be kept alive. With this purpose I bring a union created of compassion to form a new, divine seed. Until the creation of the seed occurs, what you potentially are cannot become. And, if this potential remains unrealized, life stagnates, which brings about death."

"So, if I am to understand your meaning," I respond, "you are bringing a birth to us. This birth redeems the closed system and gives hope to life's evolution. You say you catalyze the process. I see you as a midwife."

My ally excitedly responds, "Yes, I come to give birth to Life, by returning the ecstatic to existence. Your befriending me opens you to an experience of Life as a real, living essence, to which you can relate. My ultimate goal is to bring divinity out of hiding and into an unimaginable relationship with itself."

Bewildered by my ally's words, I dream that night of allies chained within a cave just waiting for their human counterpart to free them. The freeing simply requires the act of befriending. Yet, in the dream, there is a lot of reluctance, due to fear. When the fear is overcome, the *person* as well as the ally is brought out of hiding into a shared union.

When I return to my dialogue with Yiam, several experiences of union transpire. I feel ourselves as two different incense smokes mingling and as two colors coming together to create a new color. We become a marbled cake, one the white part, and one the pink. We exist as a mixture of salt and sugar only distinguishable by taste. And, we embody the properties of particle and wave to become light. We come together as something new, with a new center released from our previous identities of being only this or that.

"I shall wake the passive eternal to the discovery of its Self with our union born of love and knowledge of life's need to be fed the Light. Consciousness sustains life. Time brings me forth to resuscitate and restore what has only until now been a potential for the Divine. And that is a condition of wholeness bound by relatedness," quietly whispers my guest.

"This confuses me when you speak of divine potential and divine wholeness. I always assumed that these properties were inherent in the Divine. To allude to the fact that we humans have an integral part in the process seems blasphemous."

"So it must," replies my guest. "Therefore, I come to force a focus upon the 'human-Divine' so that God might live and grow. You were created of divine substance, as you know from all your creation stories. What meaning does this have for you?"

With this question Yiam touches my heart and I am stricken with an intense experience of twin-ness to God such as the salt and sugar mix or the new colored solution. It no longer matters who speaks the words, "I am of you as you are of me," as the truth is spoken by human or God. And God and I become "Real" in that moment. Something deeply seated within me screams out against accepting this humanly divine equality with God. I feel that I transgress an ancient taboo.

"Ah," sighs my ally. "You must struggle against this ancient taboo of seeing your true nature by acceptance of the profound heartfelt experiences and acquired knowledge of your inalienable right to existence, life and love. As you experience your own creation from Creation, you will know in the deepest, most unshakable sense that you indeed exist in meaningful, equal relationship to the Divine."

"Your purpose sounds shocking in the suggestion of changing our whole psychic framework. Is this really possible, and how am I to conceive of such a reality?" I inquire.

Typical of our dialoging, a visual meditation seems to spring upon me, a gift from Yiam. I dive into a great body of water descending to the bottom. When I arrive at the muddy bottom I stub my toe on a broken object, drawing blood. I pick up the object to discard it and my ally sings out that our relationship will clear away all objects from the bottom of this water. I see instantly the truth of this as if looking into the future with the mud being completely clear of all debris and I come upon the smooth, clean, hard rock surface beneath the mud. I feel this and know it to be the very outer edge of creation. Looking all about me, the clearness and clarity sweeps me like a current into an ecstatic state of wholeness and wellness. And I experience a complete absence of fear in the total presence of Being.

"Tell me more of your purpose with relationship," I ask.

"The relationship I bring is not of a usury nature for power, knowledge or blinding enlightenment, but rather one to free you from dogma so that you can grow and ever evolve. This relationship also frees me to evolve with you in the transformations. Relationship as a union of you and I in one new body with separate consciousness causes a paradox. Comfort with this paradox brings freedom and active living. By 'active living' I mean having the ability to be related to wholeness, which necessitates an ego or consciousness. Maintaining differentiation keeps ego awareness intact. In turn, that which it is aware of stays alive. If either of us dissolves into the other, the other becomes nonexistent and, therefore, non-relational and unknowable."

Responding to a churning feeling, I ask, "Are you suggesting a mutual need and dependency? Collectively, dependency has a very negative judgmental value. People struggle against this in order to be 'independent,' and there are numerous therapies and self-help books assisting in this goal of independence."

"Such misunderstanding." says Yiam. "The struggle against dependency keeps you from authentic relatedness, just as being succumbed by dependency also prevents authentic relatedness. We have a mutual need and a mutual dependency. This mutual neediness of the individual and the Divine, when felt, appreciated, and embraced, opens all to mutual change on a path of eternal incarnations. I come here due to our mutual need. I depend upon you, whom I guide, just as you depend upon me, your guide."

Comprehension slowly descends upon me as I experience an intense closeness with my guest. Our hearts quite literally touch, sending forth waves of profound love, bathing every cell of my body. This love feeds both hearts, and I instantly know and feel that for either of us to separate would be our death for we would live without life. "Your purpose is purely for relationship," I sigh.

"Yes, for a relationship that transfigures both partners. I come to bring creation and non-creation into a relational state of continual transformations. Our friendship will grow ever closer so that both of us are drawn into a union of living, life essence, fulfilling the intended potential of Juglan, which has not yet become. This relationship will bring about the fulfillment of a person's capacity for consciousness of and participation in a whole divinity. And in that fulfillment, I, too, am completed. Of course, to do this, I must somehow get you people out of your shamed hiding," states my guest.

"Whatever do you mean by our 'shamed hiding'? You are again speaking to me in riddles," I stammer.

Barely is my comment spoken when a vision from Yiam comes. The vision depicts the condition in which humans feel themselves. A strong light blows open all the doors of thousands of toilet stalls, exposing a scared, shamed people in hiding. The ally comes to free the people from their assumed position to stand equal before the gods.

"This state of shamed hiding, I am sure, must stem from the many denigrating creation stories of humankind. I am intent on pushing you out from the shadow of the Divine so that you can know your Self and God with renewed clarity. In this I shall free you from all fears, which will eradicate the "power" archetype that exists as a reaction to fear. This as yet unimaginable state of being is like living in eternal spring," emphasizes my ally. And Yiam gives me a kiss.

This kiss fills me with the taste of eternal spring that is fully pregnant and bursting forth with Life. This Life exists without Death. The cycles of time are broken. The heat of summer that wilts is absent. The decline that accompanies fall will never come and, therefore, winter recedes from all memory. My guest brings me this promise of spring through our mutually fulfilled bond of friendship and love.

I startle out of this gifted kiss with an urgent question: "How do you establish a permanent relationship to the ally once the ally has introduced itself to you?"

"Your question, which comes straight from the heart, I shall gladly answer," offers Yiam. "Of course, you must be willing to come out from hiding in order to respond to the invitation of friendship and love. And then, take my hand, and allow yourself to be guided."

"This seems easy enough," I quickly interject.

"Really?" whispers my ally. "Can you let go of thinking that you know what's right? Can you allow yourself to be guided when you need it, not when you want it? Can you step into the unknown and non-experienced without holding onto the familiar? Do you possess the humility to allow yourself to trust me? You must allow yourself to be stripped of knowledge in order to experience what you do not know."

"My heart screams out to trust and I intend to follow my heart on this matter. The public will deem this as crazy and my colleagues will accuse me of exalting the imagination. So be it!" I declare.

"The path of Self-discovery in individuation upon which you stride opens the way for us. You are accustomed to the struggle of a given, known reality against a reality that has yet to exist in the process of your ego making room for the Self as the two come into relationship. This happens only by accepting your experience of the extraordinary. This center or relationship to the Self, which you create, provides the portal through which our hands and heart touch. However, this touching will rip away at your long-upheld truths and will enlighten the meaning of having to leave home. Can you surrender your comfort zone by taking your hands from your face, by coming out of hiding and then looking into the eyes of your guest?" challenges Yiam.

Immediately, I recall a dream in which I lay with my hands covering my face upon the tundra beyond the warm, family-filled cottage. The wolf licking my face invites me into relationship with it. Fear dissolves in the wake of love. To embrace the wolf, I knowingly must give up all that the cottage represents. This includes my identity of myself as a mother and all the other roles that I play. My idea of success in the achievement of the cozy home must be abandoned. My ego will be shaken loose from its many beliefs, which keep it bound to the cottage.

Looking back across the tundra toward the cottage, I feel the death that precedes new life. I see the attraction of the warm cottage as an archetypal lure with a powerful pressure to yield to it as if to a "herd instinct."

"Let me set you free from this obsessive archetypal attraction," offers the ally. "Imagine dismantling an atom so that all its parts are no longer habitually related, thus allowing a totally new alignment to occur. In other words, what you know of life gives way to an entirely new experience of life. You affect the psyche rather than being affected by the psyche. You can choose between a personal mythic path or stay with a collectively given path. Search your heart and embrace its desire."

In a vision, I see a person splashing about the top of the water, changing the water's appearance for a brief moment and not moving very efficiently. Another person kicks deeply underwater, creating a forceful current, and moving strongly through the water. The first person is likened to the brief, quick-fix therapies and the second person to individuation where the change seen on top happens because of a change from underneath, the underneath representing the unconscious. The ally is asking that I commit to a deep-water dive to the very bottom so that the completely unseen bottom can be transformed. This unseen bottom surface compares to the collective unconscious or the structure that encloses the psyche. This image of a deepwater dive to the bottom triggers fond childhood memories of summers spent exploring underwater. My passion and curiosity for such alien newness fires my choice for the journey toward relationship with my guest.

"Yes, I feel the desire from my heart to come into relationship with you. I extend my hand in search of friendship."

"You realize," cautions my ally, "that desire will not be enough to keep our friendship intact. Guts, tenaciousness, honesty, and, most of all, absolute trust will be necessary for us to embrace in a loving relationship. Already I feel your fear of becoming unaccepted and misunderstood in your world. Desire to 'fit in' or fear of not 'fitting in' bars your heart from me. I can feel you struggle with the inherent human identification of unworthiness of and inferiority to the Divine. Shed this yoke of unworthiness, as well as those of arrogance and inflation. Fight against that monster called "control." For these are the things that challenge the greatest of intentions. Friendship between us is not a spectator affair. You must participate with me to pull down the barriers between us."

Panic seeps in as I listen to Yiam. "Go to my heart. Feel from my heart. See through my heart." I repeat this litany to calm myself. I know that we protect ourselves from the experience of the heart by adhering to the rational as the only voice of truth. And Yiam just stated that trust must prevail. "I assume that trust comes from the heart?"

"Yes, trust reflects a faith in one's own gut feeling of an experience. It overcomes the dogma that control will protect the practitioner from chaos or the unknown. And it demonstrates an ability to detach from 'shoulds' such as 'I should do this,' or 'I should do that.' Hold to your desire and, with great effort, you will acquire the trust necessary for our relationship, which will dismantle, rearrange, and realign your very existence."

I absent-mindedly reply, "While you were talking, a passage from the New Testament came to me. The devil's tempting of Christ in the desert reminds me to trust. As Christ said: 'Do not test your God!' People become easy prey to the devil's bargaining: give me happiness and I'll believe. Give me health and I'll believe. Give me wealth and I'll believe. Give me power and I'll believe. These demands ask for assurance and payment in exchange for the relationship and reflect a basic mistrust and disbelief in a bond of mutual love. The demands also depict that insidious need for control."

"Control," continues my ally, "impedes the heart and therefore love. Consider control to be a false god that promises to protect from death. Humans are taught to worship control. Do you recall your third grade friend's death?"

A forgotten memory floods my heart. A third grade friend dies when his bike strikes a brick wall. The adult response to my shock at losing a young friend revolves around control. If he had had better control of his bike, he would not be dead. We are inundated with ways of controlling our lives in order to avoid an "early" death. So, surely, letting go of control will mean instant death or, at the least, chaos. Avoiding death through the aid of the false god, Control, completely interferes with embracing Trust. So, how does one give up control for trust when trust must be needed to give up control?

Aware of my question, the ally answers, "The experiences I offer to you in meditation will, in time, dismantle the false god. Listen, hear, and feel what occurs in your meditation. Avoid concretizing their irrational nature, which only becomes an act of controlling the experience. Tenacious attachment to a non-experienced, taught belief robs you of knowing the truth. Let yourself be emptied of early learning and the prejudices of collective thinking."

I see a row of "me's" from birth to the absolute present and experience them all strung together into the very moment. All that comprises me is present. The past rolls into the present, that would become the future. The present and future depend upon my past, which is shaped so much by personal experiences being redefined to fit the collectively acceptable experience. In this way, compartmentalizing into preexisting truths and ideas subtly eliminates anything new. My ally cuts my string and all of the "me's" spill forth as I scream in shocked awareness of the realigning and relearning that will transpire.

My ally calmly explains, "You must withstand this sensation of being torn asunder in order to experience the unimaginable with me. There is much beyond the imagination! And when you come to realize this, you will be prepared to accept my alien-ness."

I laugh to myself in recalling a scene from *Alice in Wonderland*. The queen asked Alice about her ability to imagine the unimaginable. Of course, Alice does not do such a thing, at which point the queen explains that she always spends time imagining the unimaginable before breakfast. This exchange emphasizes Alice's stifled experiences and close-mindedness. I am beginning to feel like Alice.

The ally continues, "In these experiences, you will come to know truths, which will challenge your intellectual understanding of things. These experiences fortify convictions of the heart necessary to overcome the fear of transgressing the collective truths, that is, of not being adapted. This fear prevents you from letting go of knowledge that contradicts what you experience. Therefore, you must hold to the inner journey experiences rather than to the word of others. Again, our relationship demands adherence to one's heartfelt encounters, which will conflict with your intellectually acquired knowledge. So often you throw away what is experienced, when it goes against an assumed truth. Let your heart overthrow your indoctrination of non-experienced truths. And this means giving up the idea of a "right" way to do things. A stage neither needs to be set nor a script memorized in order to meet me. We come together through the heart. Trust is born there and control forsaken."

I begin to feel heavy with the sense of this relationship not being possible, and of my being unable to accomplish the connection. A litany of self-criticisms and doubts run through my head, crippling my focus on the ally.

"Watch out!" shouts Yiam. "You are under attack. Anything that steps between you and me must be identified and named so that you do not become consumed by it. Remember that the archetypes' jealousy seeks to destroy our friendship."

An unsolicited experience of solid ecstasy seeps through my body, returning my heart to my guest. I feel myself born from myself as equal with the self-creating, the force of life, so that the relationship with Yiam is devoid of any hierarchy. We are partners. I become an "other" to the ally so that relationship might exist. I know at once that relationship is the Elixir of Life. Relationship becomes a third element from the product of the two of us, which is greater than and different from its parts, yet unable to exist without its parts, the ally and myself. A living trinity now exists. The interaction of Yiam and myself produces the third, our relationship, which nourishes both of us, thus becoming the parent of the parents. Love erupts in every cell of our body. Love binds this relationship.

"Our relationship must be without an agenda," confides Yiam. "Don't pray to me for accomplishments and things and good feelings. Rather, come to me in partnership and love that we might give birth to

Life's newness. Seek not power or enlightenment. Instead, seek only my heart for a relationship of love that provides eternal growth. Just as a seed naturally matures into the flower meant to be, so also will we. Take heed of the lessons of China's folktales in which ill fate befalls the human or the "spirit" involved in self-indulgent pursuits. I offer you an opportunity of unimaginable companionship."

"How can such companionship be achieved?" I quickly ask.

I become immediately aware of my heartbeat as its pattern grips my attention. I am breathing and the ally is breathing in synch with me. The ally is breathing and I am breathing in synch with it. My heart sings to it as its heart sings to me. Then we feel each other's rhythms give way to a new, unique, single synchronization of breathing. My ally whispers the word "gating" to me, which I immediately feel is a description of our newly achieved movement together. I realize to my utter amazement that gating happens through trust. I trust! However did this occur?

Laughing, my ally responds, "Experience after experience of ecstatic encounters with unconditional love eventually gives way to trust. This trust allows the mingled union of you and I. Imagine a field of wheat and rice planted next to each other. A few grains begin to mix at the border of the fields. As neither grain is destroyed they continue to cross and mix in each other's field until thoroughly mixed into one large field where they grow in abundance."

I feel a surprising insight creeping into my consciousness. "This story you tell alludes to the fact that you, too, must trust or that you also have fears of being hurt by me. In that case, the issue is not so one-sided and makes it seem much more like a mutual seeking and meeting as two living strangers forge a friendship of eternal love."

My guest-turned-friend, Yiam, slowly releases his breath and quietly exclaims, "Yes, that is what I mean by an equal partnership! I, too, risk myself in reaching across the tremendous boundary of the Archetype of Humanness in order to secure our relationship. Once we acknowledge each other, if you abandon me, I die. The power of our attraction and the sustainment of our relationship lie in our mutual need, reward and transformation, which sums up the concept in evolution that attains to the goal of self-fulfillment. The idea of equality counters the notion of a "father" God or a "mother" God, who might provide parenting for that eternal child relationship. Letting go of such an archetypal pattern brings about true maturity, indicative of the mutual responsibility necessary for the continual unfolding of life's very essence. We are in this together. You affect me and I affect you."

A profound love sweeps through me, seemingly from nowhere and in response to nothing that I have done or said or thought. Love pervades as a thing of itself and simply exists to be tasted. The effect of our relationship I know in the depth of my soul is this living love. It heals anything that might need to be healed, leaving me with an absolute peace filled with the surging energy of becoming and growth. Such is our attraction. "How do I help you across the boundary?"

"Grab hold of an image or idea tenaciously, thus pulling it into form. Pulling something into form is to make it real. The image of me or the idea of me found in dreams or stories must be held onto while you tease the image/idea into reality by relating to it." The ally continues, "You exist in a reflected world that you assume is real. Even the creation stories at times say that this world is a reflection of the heaven or other world from which the creator originated. As a reflection, it is not the actual object. The real object exists on the other side of the psyche. Humans are born into a unique position of responsibility for being able to grab hold of the 'reflected' through conscious focus to pull the actual object from its reflection. You see, the reflection of a reflection is the actual object. I am the reflection of the reflection of the Absolute Divine. You are the medium through which the Divine is made real, just as I am the medium through which the Human is made real."

I remain speechless for some time as I plunge into an experience of Yiam's words. I feel immensely awed at the ramifications and magnitude of ally work in birthing the substantial Real from the not-yet-Real. I have no ability with words to describe the "seeing" that occurs through his words.

I now know that boundary crossing and mutual relatedness with the guest require the following tools: gating, moving in unison with the ally, active imagination and meditation. With these tools, I discovered a living gift beyond human imagination and a gift of total, unconditional, loving acceptance in an eternal relationship of divineness. The achievement of such a gift comes only through the risked experience of the heart, rather than the safe intellectualism of the mind. I shall never feel alone! I shall never cease living! Thank you, Yiam, for your arrival.

CONCLUSION

YOU WHO HUNGER for spiritual fulfillment may now find some hope and direction in the spiritual paradigm that we offer in this book. The current predicament of the human being has been described as one of a confined existence, severed from the Divine. However, in our model of successive transformations, we each possess the potential to redeem ourselves *and* the Divine. This potential rests on the formation of the human-Divine center, our divinity, and on the ally, an incarnation of the Divine. We are at an opportune time for spiritual growth, as a result of our expanding consciousness and thirst for personally meaningful experiences of God. This book presents a new spiritual model that emphasizes our active participation in the healing and evolution of the Divine.

The idea of a dismembered Divine, although it may violate the accepted, collective image of a perfect God, comes directly from the symbolism within mythology. Mythology has been instrumental in laying a foundation for the idea of a split in the Divine. It has also been used to delineate the concepts of both the psychoid, the world beyond the psyche, and the ally. And, it describes the creation of human beings for the purpose of meeting God's needs. However, our purpose is not generally discussed as one of helping God to become whole. This new paradigm does address both the individual's and ally's participation in a series of transformational unions that ultimately heal this split. Through these unions, God and humans fully become what they were intended to be.

The first stage of union is individuation. C. G. Jung made a life's work of developing this process. This stage is essential in establishing a mature, intact ego, which is necessary for moving forward on this spiritual path. Unfortunately, many of us today assume that individuation is an end in itself. We view the individuation process simply as a beginning to our spiritual evolution. This evolution is about the expansion of consciousness beyond the boundaries of the psyche and the union of this expanded consciousness with the ally and God. Through ally work, the created human-Divine center unites with the God-Divine center to form a new center, the Divine-Divine. The ally, who mediates this process, then pours itself into this center for the ultimate transformation of the individual, God, and the ally into the manifest Divine. From here, our evolution of consciousness and soul is set free to grow eternally.

Our model of spiritual transitions hinges on a relationship with the ally. Symbolism from alchemy, in particular the genius, has been used to define the nature of the ally. Alchemy symbolism also has contributed to the development of guidelines for establishing a relationship with the ally from its beginning to the deepest states of ecstatic union. In this relationship, the ally functions as our guide for the transformations, as the medium in which the transformational unions take place, and as the goal itself, since it, too, manifests through the successive stages. The ally, however, is not an angel. By now, you have acquired an understanding of the differences between ally and angel. The primary difference is the fact that angels are not involved with the transformation of the individual, God, or itself, whereas transformation is the primary agenda of the ally.

We are generally drawn into ally work by numinous dream images or psychoidal experiences that stir our search for the understanding of the mystical. The new spiritual model presented in this book draws us onto a unique path in which we experience Divine images of a very personal nature. These experiences often have a more powerful affect than the traditional, collective images. There is a sense transferred from these images that God needs us as an equal partner in order for It, as well as ourselves, to become whole. As presented in the new myth of Juglan, we are naturally created as the identical twin of the God-Divine and are, therefore, naturally Its equal partner. The partnership that each of us forms with God produces an indescribable experience of unconditional love. It also brings about a wholly, new, transformed existence. We establish such a partnership through the technique of active imagination. C. G. Jung resurrected this technique, which is probably as old as humanity. Active imagination opens the door for each of us to experience not only the psyche, but also, the psychoid. It is our hope that the example found in this book of active imagination with the ally will instill a desire to take this new path.

Since we have found this new model to already be emerging in people's dreams, it is possible that you have already come to identify with our concept of the ally from a personal experience. The concept and construct that we offer has been the result of our own experiences, the experiences of those with whom we work, and the respectful study of many earlier traditions. Because it is both an intellectual and experiential model, it can speak to your heart and soul.

Through your passion and willingness to put forth effort, you will experience success along this new spiritual path of healing. You will also reap numerous reward along the way, particularly in a deeply rooted sense of well-being. The path does, however, require focus, intent, and trust. You must learn to trust in your "imagination" experiences since the successive stages of spiritual transformation come only through the heart. When you are able to open your heart—to feel, and to trust—you will come to know the ally as a living gift beyond human imagination and will experience the ecstatic transformations of healing. We are challenged by an awakened sense of our responsibility to the work for the evolution of consciousness and Divine wholeness. This is not an easy challenge, and it demands a courageousness that will be rewarded with the gift of spiritual renewal. Without our human involvement, the Divine has no chance of healing its dismemberment. Our new spiritual paradigm thus elevates the significance of our existence.

NOTES

CHAPTER I

1 Quoted in Aniela Jaffé, *Jung's Last Years* (Dallas: Spring Publications, 1970), p. 12. Brackets mine.

2 Joseph Campbell, *Power of Myth* (New York: Doubleday, 1988), p. 42.

3 Richard Aldington and Delano Ames, trans., *New Larousse Encyclopedia of Mythology* (London: Hamlyn Publishing, 1959), pp. 248-251.

4 Marie-Louise von Franz, *Creation Myths* (Dallas: Spring Publications, 1972), p. 163.

5 Barbara C. Sproul, *Primal Myths: Creating the World* (San Francisco: Harper and Row, 1979), p. 254 (the arch is a solid rock sky vault).

6 Aldington and Ames, *New Larousse Encyclopedia of Mythology*, p. 11.

7 Sproul, *Primal Myths: Creating the World*, p. 202.

8 R. J. Stewart, *The Elements of Creation Myth* (Rockport, MA: Element Books, 1989), p. 77.

9 Genesis I: 1-31. This and further biblical references are from Alexander Jones, gen. ed., *The Jerusalem Bible* (New York: Doubleday, 1966). Future references will cite only book, chapter, and verse.

10 Paul Deussen, *Philosophy of the Upanishads* (New York: Dover Publications, 1966), p. 191.

11 James Robinson, *The Nag Hammadi Library* (San Francisco: HarperSanFrancisco, 1981), p. 162-179.

12 Robinson, *The Nag Hammadi* Library. p. 165.

13 Vivian Thompson, *Hawaiian Myths of Earth, Sea and Sky* (Honolulu: University of Hawaii Press, 1988), p. 14.

14 C. G. Jung, *Mysterium Coniunctionis, Collected Works*, vol. 14, R. F. C. Hull, trans., Bollingen Series XX (Princeton: Princeton University Press, 1977), § 759.

15 Idries Shah, *The Way of the Sufi* (New York: E. P. Dutton and Co., 1970), p. 72.

16 Tom Lowenstein, "The Circle of Heaven" in *Time Life Books: Mother Earth, Father Sky: Native American Myth* (London: Duncan Baird, 1997), p. 53.

17 C. G. Jung, *Aion, Collected Works*, vol. 9ii, R. F. C. Hull, trans., Bollingen Series XX (Princeton: Princeton University Press, 1968), § 50.

18 Frank Waters, *Book of the Hopi* (New York: Penguin, 1963), pp. 3–22.

19 Marvin Meyer, ed., *The Ancient Mysteries: A Source Book: Sacred Texts of the Mystery Religions of the Ancient Mediterranean World* (San Francisco: HarperSanFrancisco, 1987), pp. 215–218. Brackets mine.

20 E. A. Budge, trans., *The Egyptian Book of the Dead* (New York: Dove Publications, 1967), p. lxvi.

21 Budge, *The Egyptian Book of the Dead*, p. lxxiii.

22 David Guss, trans., "Watunna: Mitologia Makiritare," in *Parabola*, vol. 11, no. 2, 1977, pp. 56–65.

23 Matthew 10: 34–36.

24 S. H. Hooke, *Middle Eastern Mythology* (London: Penguin, 1963), pp. 57–58.

25 Genesis: 3: 22–23.

26 Raymond Van Over, *Sun Songs: Creation Myths from Around the World* (New York: New American Library, 1980), p. 91.

27 Italo Calvino, *Italian Folktales*, George Martin, trans. (New York: Harcourt, Brace Jovanovich, 1980), pp. 77–79.

28 Yei Theodora Ozaki, "Urashima Taro, The Fisher Lad," in *Japanese Fairy Tales* (New York: A. L. Burt Co., 1903), pp. 25–42.

CHAPTER 2

1 C. G. Jung, *The Structure and Dynamics of the Psyche, Collected Works*, vol. 8, R. F. C. Hull, trans., Bollingen Series XX (Princeton: Princeton University Press, 1969), § 431.

2 Aniela Jaffé, *Jung's Last Years* (Dallas: Spring Publications, 1971), p. 170.

3 For the purpose of this book, God's manifest Self will be referred to as the God-Divine center.

4 C. G. Jung, *Mysterium Coniunctionis, Collected Works*, vol. 14, R. F. C. Hull, trans., Bollingen Series XX (Princeton: Princeton University Press, 1970), § 711. Further references to this volume will be cited as *CW14*.

5 For the purpose of this book, human manifest Self will be referred to as the human-Divine center.

6 Richard Aldington and Delano Ames, trans., *New Larousse Encyclopedia of Mythology* (London: Hamlyn, 1959), p. 374. Kriṣna is the human incarnation of the god Viṣnu. Ṣiva is one of the Hindu gods.

7 J. Hackin, *Asiatic Mythology* (New York: Crescent Books, 1963), p. 222.

8 For the purpose of this book, the latent Psychoid Self will be referred to as the Divine-Divine center.

9 For the purpose of this book, the manifest Psychoid Self will be referred to as EO, or the Luminous Tree. Webster's Dictionary defines EO as "to dawn or to shine."

10 C. G. Jung, *The Archetypes and The Collective Unconscious, Collected Works*, vol. 9i, R F. C. Hull, trans., Bollingen Series XX (Princeton: Princeton University Press, 1969), § 198.

CHAPTER 3

1 Hyemeyohsts Storm, *Seven Arrows* (New York: Ballantine Books, 1972), p. 68–85.

2 Mike Ashley, ed., *The Giant Book of Myths and Legends* (New York: Barnes & Noble, 1995), p. 47–53.

3 C. G. Jung, *The Structure and Dynamics of the Psyche, Collected Works*, vol. 8, § 111 .

4 Carlos Castaneda, *The Eagle's Gift* (New York: Pocket Books, 1981), p. 173.

5 R. J. Stewart, *The Elements of Creation Myth* (Rockport, MA: Element Books, 1989), p. 84–87.

6 J. E. Cirlot, *A Dictionary of Symbols* (New York: Philosophical Library, 1971), p. 91.

7 Kachina, from American Indian, is a wooden replica of a spirit or deity.

8 Swani Prabhavananda and Frederick Manchester, *The Upanishads: Breath of the Eternal* (New York: New American Library, 1948), p. 20.

9 Lucie Lamy, *Egyptian Mysteries* (New York: Crossroad, 1981), p. 25.

10 H. R. Ellis Davidson, *Myths and Symbols in Pagan Europe* (Syracuse: University Press, 1988), p. 175.

11 Stewart, *The Elements of Creation Myth*, p. 47.

12 Marie-Louise von Franz, *Shadow and Evil in Fairytales* (Dallas: Spring Publications, 1983), p. 209.

13 Stewart, *The Elements of Creation Myth*, p. 57, 101.

14 Von Franz, *Creation Myths* (Dallas: Spring Publications, 1983), p. 39.

15 Jean Chevalier and Alain Gheerbrant, *The Penguin Dictionary of Symbols* (Syracuse: University Press, 1988), p. 702.

16 Hamilton Tyler, *Pueblo Gods & Myths* (Norman, OK: University of Oklahoma Press, 1964), p. 105.

17 Jung, *CW 14*, § 472.

18 Jung, *CW 14*, § 484.

CHAPTER 4

1 See Jeffrey Raff, *Jung and the Alchemical Imagination* (York Beach, ME: Nicolas-Hays, 2000).

2 Antoine Faivre and Jacob Needleman, eds. Modern Esoteric Spirituality (New York: Crossroad, 1995), p. xv.

3 Deborah Harkness, *John Dee's Conversations with Angels* (Cambridge, England: Cambridge University Press, 1999), p. 4.

4 Harkness, *Conversations*, p. 11.

5 Harkness, *Conversations*, p. 43.

6 Harkness, *Conversations*, p. 47.

7 Rudolf Steiner, *Angels* (London: Rudolf Steiner Press, 1996), p. 10.

8 Steiner, *Angels*, p. 21.

9 Steiner, *Angels*, p. 22.

10 Steiner, *Angels*, p. 39.

11 Steiner. *Angels*, P. 63.

12 Terry Lynn Taylor, *Messengers of Light* (Novato, CA: H. J. Kramer, 1990), p. xvi.

13 Taylor, *Messengers*, p. 5.

14 Taylor, *Messengers*, p. 13.

15 Taylor, *Messengers*, p. 63.

16 Henry Corbin, *Avicenna and the Visionary Recital* (Ann Arbor: UMI Books on Demand, 2000), p. 20. Italics are in the original.

17 Corbin, *Avicenna*, p. 79.

18 William C. Chittick, *The Sufi Path of Knowledge* (Albany: SUNY Press, 1989), p. x.

19 Henry Corbin, *The Man of Light in Iranian Sufism* (New Lebanon, NY: Omega Publications, 1994), p.11.

20 Quoted in Corbin, *Man of Light*, p. 17.

21 Quoted in Corbin, *Man of Light*, p. 21.

22 Corbin, *Man of Light*, p. 25.

CHAPTER 5

1 Jeffrey Raff, *Jung and the Alchemical Imagination* (York Beach, ME: Nicolas-Hays, 2000), p. 220 *ff.*

2 Ali Puli, *The Center of Nature Concentrated* (Edmonds, WA: The Alchemical Press, 1988), p. 17.

3 C. G. Jung, *Aion, Collected Works*, vol. 9ii, , R. F. C. Hull, trans., Bollingen Series XX (Princeton: Princeton University Press, 1970), §265.

4 C. G. Jung, *Alchemical Studies. Collected Works*, vol. 13, R. F. C. Hull, trans., Bollingen Series XX (Princeton: Princeton University Press, 1970), § 283. Further references will be cited as *CW 13*.

5 C. G. Jung, *CW 13*, § 282.

6 C. G. Jung, *Mysterium Coniunctionis, Collected Works*, vol. 14, R. F. C. Hull, trans., Bollingen Series XX (Princeton: Princeton University Press, 1989), § 658. Further references will be cited as *CW 14*.

7 Ioan P. Couliano, *Eros and Magic in the Renaissance*. (Chicago: University of Chicago Press, 1987). p. 221.

8 Oswald Croll, *Philosophy Reformed and Improved in Four Profound Tractates*, H. Prinnell, trans. (London: M. S. for Lodowik Lloyd, 1657), p. 71.

9 Croll, *Philosophy Reformed*, p. 73.

10 C. G. Jung, *Psychology and Alchemy, Collected Works*, vol. 12, R. F. C. Hull trans., Bollingen Series XX (Princeton University Press, 1977), § 400.

11 C. G. Jung, *The Archetypes and the Collective Unconscious, Collected Works*, vol. 9i, R. F. C. Hull, trans., Bollingen Series XX (Princeton: Princeton University Press, 1969), § 393.

12 Quoted in William C. Chittick, *Imaginal Worlds* (Albany, NY: S.U.N.Y. Press, 1994), p. 94.

13 C. G. Jung, *Memories, Dreams and Reflections* (New York: Vintage Books, 1963), p. 183.

14 Martinus Rulandus, *A Lexicon of Alchemy or Alchemical Dictionary* (Kila, MT: Kessinger, n.d.), p. 226.

15 C. G. Jung, *Psychology and Alchemy*, § 394.

16 L.G. Kelly, *Basil Valentine: His Triumphant Chariot of Antimony with Annotations of Theodore Kirkringius (1678)*, English Renaissance Hermeticism, vol. 3 (New York: Garland Publishing Co., 1990), p. 7.

17 Croll, *Philosophy Reformed*, pp. 22-23.

18 William R. Newman, *Gehennical Fire* (Cambridge, MA: Harvard University Press, 1994), p. 65. Brackets mine.

19 Henry Cornelius Agrippa, *Three Books of Occult Philosophy*, Llewellyn's Sourcebook Series, Donald Tyson ed., James Freake, trans. (St. Paul, MN: Llewellyn, 1995), p. 525.

20 Quoted in Thomas Moore, *The Planets Within* (Hudson, NY: Lindisfarne Press, 1990), p. 55.

21 Croll, *Philosophy Reformed*, p. 67.

22 Paracelsus, "Concerning the Nature of Things," in *The Hermetic and Alchemical Writings of Paracelsus*, A.E. Waite, ed. (Kila, MT: Kessinger, reprint of 1910 edition), pp. 124–125.

23 Paracelsus, "Concerning the Nature of Things," pp. 124–125.

24 Paracelsus, "Concerning the Nature of Things," pp. 124–125.

25 Jung, *CW 14*, § 490

26 Jeffrey Raff, *Jung and the Alchemical Imagination*, p. 143.

27 Jung, *CW 13*, § 162.

28 Quoted in Mircea Eliade, *Shamanism*, Willard R. Trask, trans. Bollingen Series LXXVI (Princeton: Princeton University Press, 1974), pp. 60–61.

29 Henry Corbin, *The Man of Light in Iranian Sufism* (New Lebanon, NY: Omega Publications, 1994), p. 14.

30 Betty Jo Teeter Dobbs, *The Janus Faces of Genius* (Cambridge, England: Cambridge University Press, 1991), p. 40.

31 Jung, *CW 13*, § 256.

32 Croll, *Philosophy Reformed*, p. 67.

33 John Pordage, *Philosophisches Send-Schreiben* quoted in Johannes Fabricius, *Alchemy* (London: Diamond Books, 1976), pp. 190–191.

34 John Trinick, *The Fire-Tried Stone* (Cornwall, UK: Wordens of Cornwall Limited, 1967), p. 19.

CHAPTER 6

1 C. G. Jung, *The Structure and Dynamics of the Psyche* (Princeton: Princeton University Press, 1969), § 400.

2 William C. Chittick, *Imaginal Worlds* (Albany: S.U.N.Y. Press, 1994), p. 59.

3 Chittick, *Imaginal Worlds*, p. 94.

4 Jeffrey Raff "The Felt Vision," in Donald Sander and Steven Wong, eds, *The Sacred Heritage* (New York: Routledge, 1977).

5 Marie-Louise von Franz, *Individuation in Fairytales* (Zurich: Spring Publications, 1977), pp. 103–104.

6 Oswald Croll, *Philosophy Reformed and Improved in Four Profound Tractates*, H. Pinnell, trans. (London: M.S. for Lodowik Lloyd, 1657), p. 67.

BIBLIOGRAPHY

Agrippa, Henry Cornelius. *Three Books of Occult Philosophy*. Donald Tyson, ed., James Freake, trans. Llewellyn's Sourcebook Series. St. Paul, MN: Llewellyn Publications, 1995.

Aldington, Richard and Delano Ames, trans. *New Larousse Encyclopedia of Mythology*. London: Hamlyn, 1959.

Ashley, Mike, ed. *The Giant Book of Myths and Legends*. New York: Barnes and Noble, 1995.

Budge, E. A. Wallis, trans. *The Egyptian Book of the Dead*. New York: Dover Publications, 1967.

Calvino, Italo. *Italian Folktales*. George Martin, trans. New York: Harcourt, Brace, Jovanovich, 1980.

Campbell, Joseph. *The Power of Myth*. New York: Doubleday, 1988.

Castaneda, Carlos. *The Eagle's Gift*. New York: Pocket Books, 1981.

Chevalier, Jean and Alain Gheerbrant. *The Penguin Dictionary of Symbols*. John Buchanan-Brown, trans. New York: Penguin Books, 1996.

Chittick, William C. *Imaginal Worlds*. Albany: S.U.N.Y. Press, 1994.

———. *The Sufi Path of Knowledge*. Albany: S.U.N.Y. Press, 1989.

Cirlot, J. E. *A Dictionary of Symbols*. New York: Philosophical Library, 1971.

Corbin, Henry. *Avicenna and the Visionary Recital.* Ann Arbor: UMI Books on Demand, 2000.

———. *The Man of Light in Iranian Sufism.* New Lebanon, NY: Omega Publications, 1994.

Ioan P. Couliano. *Eros and Magic in the Renaissance.* Chicago: University of Chicago Press, 1987.

Croll, Oswald. *Philosophy Reformed and Improved in Four Profound Tractates.* H. Prinnell, trans. London: M. S. for Lodowik Lloyd. 1657.

Davidson, H. R. Ellis. *Myths and Symbols in Pagan Europe.* Syracuse: University Press, 1988.

Deussen, Paul. *The Philosophy of the Upanishads.* New York: Dover Publications, 1966.

Dobbs, Betty Jo Teeter. *The Janus Faces of Genius.* Cambridge, England: Cambridge University Press, 1991.

Eliade, Mircea. *Shamanism.* Willard R. Trask, trans. Bollingen Series LXXVI. Princeton: Princeton University Press, 1974.

Faivre, Antoine and Jacob Needleman, eds. *Modern Esoteric Spirituality.* New York: Crossroad, 1995.

Fabricius, Johannes. *Alchemy.* London: Diamond Books, 1976.

Farmer, Penelope. *Beginnings: Creation Myths of the World.* New York: Athenium Press, 1979.

Guss, David, trans. "Watunna: Mitologia Makiritare," in *Parabola,* vol. 11, issue 2, 1977.

Hackin, J. et al. *Asiatic Mythology.* New York: Crescent Books, n.d.

Harkness, Deborah. *John Dee's Conversations with Angels.* Cambridge: Cambridge University Press, 1999.

Hooke, S. H. Middle *Eastern Mythology.* London: Penguin Books, 1963.

Jaffé, Aniela. *Jung's Last Years*. Dallas: Spring Publications, 1971.

Jones, Alexander, gen. ed. *The Jerusalem Bible*. New York: Doubleday & Co., Inc., 1966.

Jung, C. G. *Alchemical Studies. Collected Works*, vol. 13. R. F. C. Hull, trans. Bollingen Series XX. Princeton: Princeton University Press, 1970.

————. *Aion. Collected Works*, vol. 9ii. R.F.C. Hull, trans. Bollingen Series XX. Princeton: Princeton University Press, 1968.

————. *The Archetypes and the Collective Unconscious. Collected Works*, vol. 9i. R.F.C. Hull, trans. Bollingen Series XX. Princeton: Princeton University Press, 1969.

————. *Memories, Dreams, and Reflections*. New York: Vintage Books, 1963.

————. *Mysterium Coninunctionis. Collected Works*, vol. 14, R. F. C. Hull, trans. Bollingen Series XX. Princeton: Princeton University Press, 1963.

————. *Psychology and Alchemy. Collected Works*, vol. 12. R. F. C. Hull, trans. Bollingen Series XX. Princeton: Princeton University Press, 1977.

————. *Psychology and Religion: West and East. Collected Works*, vol. 11. R. F. C. Hull, trans. Bollingen Series XX. Princeton: Princeton University Press, 1969.

————. *The Structure and Dynamics of the Psyche. Collected Works*, vol. 8. R. F. C. Hull, trans. Bollingen Series XX. Princeton: Princeton University Press, 1969.

Kelly, L. G. *Basil Valentine: His Triumphant Chariot of Antimony with Annotations of Theodore Kirkringius (1678)*. English Renaissance Hermeticism, vol. 13. New York: Garland Publishing, 1990.

Lamy, Lucie. *Egyptian Mysteries.* New York: Crossroad Publishing, 1981.

Lowenstein, Tom. "The Circle of heaven," in *Time Life Books: Mother Earth, Father Sky: Native American Myth.* London: Duncan Baird Publishers, 1997.

Meyer, Marvin W. *The Ancient Mysteries: A Source Book: Sacred Texts of the Mystery Religions of the Ancient Mediterranean World.* San Francisco: HarperSanFrancisco, 1987.

Moore, Thomas. *The Planets Within.* Hudson, NY: Lindisfarne Press, 1990.

Newman, William R. *Gehennical Fire.* Cambridge, MA: Harvard University Press, 1994.

Ozaki, Yei Theodora. *Japanese Fairy Tales.* New York: A. L. Burt, 1908.

Paracelsus. *The Hermetic and Alchemical Writings of Paracelsus, Part One* . A. E. Waite, ed. Kila, MT: Kessinger Publishing, 1997 reprint of 1910 edition.

Puli, Ali. *The Center of Nature Concentrated.* Edmonds, WA: Alchemical Press, 1988.

Prabhavananda, Swami and Frederick Manchester, trans. *The Upanishads: Breath of the Eternal.* New York: New American Library, 1948.

Raff, Jeffrey. *Jung and the Alchemical Imagination.* York Beach, ME: Nicolas-Hays, 2000.

Robinson, James. *The Nag Hammadi Library.* San Francisco: Harper & Row, 1981.

Rulandus, Martinus. *A Lexicon of Alchemy or Alchemical Dictionary.* Kila, MT: Kessinger Publishing, n.d.

Shah, Idries. *The Way of the Sufi.* New York: E. P. Dutton & Co., 1970.

Sproul, Barbara C. *Primal Myths: Creating the World*. San Francisco: Harper & Row, 1979.

Sander, Donald and Steven Wong, eds. *The Sacred Heritage*. New York: Routledge, 1977.

Steiner, Rudolf. *Angels*. London: Rudolf Steiner Press, 1996.

Stewart, R. J. *The Elements of Creation Myth*. Rockport, MA: Element Books, 1989.

Storm, Hyemeyohsts. *Seven Arrows*. New York: Ballantine Books, 1972.

Taylor, Terry Lynn. *Messengers of Light: The Angels' Guide to Spiritual Growth*. Novato, CA: HJ Kramer, 1990.

Thompson, Vivian L. *Hawaiian Myths of Earth, Sea, and Sky*. Honolulu: University of Hawaii Press, 1994.

Trinick, John. *The Fire-Tried Stone*. Cornwall, UK: Wordens of Cornwall, 1967.

Tyler, Hamilton. *Pueblo Gods & Myths*. Norman, OK: University of Oklahoma Press, 1964.

Van Over, Raymond. *Sun Songs: Creation Myths from Around the World*. New York: New American Library, 1980.

Von Franz, Marie-Louise. *Creation Myths*. Dallas: Spring Publications, 1983.

———. *Individuation in Fairy Tales*. Boston: Shambhala Publications, 1990.

———. *Shadow and Evil in Fairytales*. Dallas: Spring Publications, 1983.

Waters, Frank. *Book of the Hopi*. New York: Penguin Books, 1963.

INDEX

ABOUT THE AUTHORS

 JEFFREY RAFF received his B. A. from Bates College, a Master's in Psychology from the New School for Social Research, and a Ph. D. in Psychology from the Union Graduate School. He graduated as a diplomate from the C. G. Jung Institute in Zurich. He has had a private practice in Littleton, Colorado, since 1976, and teaches classes, seminars, and workshops on Jungian psychology and alchemy all over the country. Readers may contact Dr. Raff at his Web site http://www.jeffraff.com.

 LINDA BONNINGTON VOCATURA received her B. S. with Honors in Psychology from the University of Washington, and a Master's in Social Work from the University of Denver. She studied with the Inter-Regional Society of Jung in Denver, Colorado, from 1981 to 1985. She has had a private practice in Denver, Colorado, since 1981, and has presented workshops for both national and local groups on dreams, active imagination, and the ally.